commons
journal of social criticism

THE RUSSIAN INVASION AND THE UKRAINIAN LEFT:

THE STRUGGLE FOR A SOCIAL UKRAINE

Issue Editor: Stas Serhiienko
Cover: Katya Gritseva
Layout: Mariia Boiko
Author of the cover photo: Ivan Samoilov

The edition is supported by *Glänta* and Region Västra Götaland. Produced in relation to *Glänta's* journal-in-residence program in Gothenburg.

We also express our gratitude to Resistance Books for additional printing and distribution of this issue

Support *Commons*

The online journal of social criticism *Commons* is an independent non-profit edition, which exists at the expense of reader's donations and grant support. Each of your contributions promotes publications of original texts of Ukrainian authors, translations of foreign articles, as well as printing of hard copies of our issues.

https://commons.com.ua/en/donate/

We are grateful to everyone who supports our intentions to explore the world around and make it a better place!

Published by Resistance Books, London
www.resistancebooks.org; info@resistancebooks.org

ISBN 978-0-902869-48-6

Profits from the sales of this journal will go to fundraising initiatives for humanitarian relief and support of leftist and trade-unionist soldiers

CONTENTS

Editorial Foreword

The idea of creating an English-language issue of *Commons* journal has been discussed for a long time, and it became especially acute in connection with the Russian full-scale invasion and the emerging significant interest in Ukraine among foreign audiences. For various reasons we have been postponing this issue, but the idea came up again during discussions with the editorial staff of the Swedish magazine *Glänta*, which invited us to a residency in Gothenburg. They offered to help us with printing — we agreed to gather the essential materials.

The war has affected each of us. Some of our friends and relatives were under occupation, captured or killed. One of our editors volunteered to join the army, several of our authors died in action on the frontline, fighting against the aggressor. Some fled the country as refugees and together with those of us who were already abroad — joined various volunteer networks and public discussions about what has been happening. We were struggling to manage and survive — some as refugees, and others staying in Ukraine, all going through the stress and not everybody being able to handle it. Our editor, comrade and dear friend Oleksandr Kravchuk, who was just 37 years old, died in June 2023 in his sleep.

All the while, we have never stopped analyzing the unfolding events. The materials presented here are not original articles written for this issue. They are either selected texts that we have published since the beginning of the full-scale invasion on our website or publications with members of the editorial board on other resources. The main part of the issue is conventionally divided into three blocks. The first contains texts that are our intervention in the Western left's discussion on Ukraine. The second, most heterogeneous block is devoted to the experiences of war — primarily occupation and refugeeism, but also the experience of solidarity and mutual support. In this section one can also find texts about the reaction of Ukrainian leftists to the war and on the situation with Ukrainian right-wing radicals. The third and final block contains articles that criticize neoliberal solutions to the country's economic problems, calling for a just and socially oriented post-war reconstruction. The interview immediately following this foreword serves as a short presentation of our journal to a foreign audience.

We would like to thank the *Glänta* editorial team, without whose assistance this issue would not have been possible. We want to thank Katya Gritseva for the cover and Mariia Boiko for the layout of the journal. Despite the very tight deadlines they did a wonderful job.

We want to thank Ira Yatsenko, Lila Badekha and Zhenya Stepko — people from our team, without whom our work over the past year and a half would have been impossible.

We would also like to thank our comrades — trade unionists and left-wing activists from all around the globe, who have supported us during these hard times. We express our gratitude to Medico International and Rosa Luxemburg Stiftung - without their cooperation many of the texts included in this issue would not have been published.

We dedicate this issue to the memory of Ukrainian anthropologist and our author Evheny Osievsky, and to the memory of our editor, friend and comrade Oleksandr Kravchuk, without whose painstaking editorial work most of these texts would not have seen the light of day.

Interview with Commons: A Ukrainian Left-Wing Collective Intellectual

Interviewed by

Patrick Le Tréhondat

One of the paradoxes of the war in Ukraine is that some of us have discovered the existence of an active left and a critical and creative thinking in Ukraine that we (including the author of these lines) have ignored for too many years. Amongst our revelations, *Commons*, Journal of Social Criticism, is certainly one of the most important and productive places for us to understand the situation in Ukraine — and in the world. It publishes its articles in Ukrainian, English, and Russian. Today *Commons* is a reference website for critical thinking on the European left. While the site deals with issues specific to Ukraine, it is open to the world. One of its recent initiatives is the "Dialogues of the peripheries", the objective being that "resistance to the capitalist system should be a way to find alternative solutions for all countries of the global periphery. To this end, we are initiating a common independent dialogue with activists from different regions, from Latin America to East Asia." I recently had a conversation with the editorial board of *Commons*.

Patrick Le Tréhondat: Commons was founded in 2009. Under what circumstances, by whom, and why was it founded?

Commons: At that point, Ukraine already had a certain ecosystem of left-wing organizations, ranging from anarchists to various kinds of Marxists. Their activities included, e.g., a campaign against the new Labor Code and protests against real estate developers illegally seizing public space. There were also a number of left-wing online resources. Founders of *Commons*, for the most part, belonged to or sympathized with one or several of these initiatives. However, they were not satisfied with the quality of political analysis that was typical of the leftist milieu in Kyiv at that time. Many of these people were students or researchers, some already exposed to Marxist discussions and texts through Western universities, which were much more sophisticated and up to date than the texts discussed by activists in Ukraine.

So, initially these people launched a mailing list that they called "leftist thought" to hold informed politically engaged discussions. Soon they decided to start a website that would popularize global socially critical thought among a wider population. First publications were almost exclusively translations. Gradually, we started producing our own texts as well, and soon we launched a paper journal. The idea behind it was to have something akin to a proper academic journal, with peer review and high intellectual standards, but independent from all academic bureaucracy. Some of these founders are still on the team; with others we have parted ways. The paper journal does not exist anymore. But the general idea is still the same: to produce and distribute high-quality, politically engaged social analysis.

PT: More generally, in addition to denouncing the damage of the global capitalist system, it seems that you are seeking to highlight the alternatives that are being built here and now and in the more specific context of colonized societies on the periphery of the capitalist system. Is this concern an effect of the situation in Ukraine? Why?

C: It is clear that Ukraine is a peripheral country, and that this fact cannot be ignored in developing social analysis and political strategies. While the initial impulse behind *Commons* was to familiarize the post-Soviet public with Western thought, we never intended to stop at this unidirectional transmission. We learn a lot from our

Patrick Le Tréhondat is a longtime French activist, writer and a member of the French publishing house *Syllepse*

Western comrades, but we feel that they also have a lot to learn from peripheral locations of knowledge production. We also feel that we need an independent exchange of experiences and perspectives with other peripheral countries. Same goes for the revolution vs the "here and now" perspective: the two need to be combined, otherwise the anticapitalist rhetoric remains shallow and general, just as "practical solutions" do not lead us anywhere without a wider radical perspective.

PT: And so you are very interested in the situations and experiences of social movements in Latin America, Africa, Asia? This may seem paradoxical for a European country.

C: After the start of full-scale war, we realized that what we knew and published about peripheral countries was often written by Western left-wing authors, or those from the Global South who have long lived in the West. The same played out in the Ukrainian case — when attention suddenly focused on our society, those were often the Western people whose perspective on the Russian invasion was the loudest and often the most valued. Even if they had never dealt with the Ukrainian context before. Unfortunately, this was also true for leftist discussion, though leftists are supposed to care about hierarchies, power relations, context, and representations. At the same time, the war contributed to the emergence of new contacts with leftists from all over the world. We decided that a more direct dialogue with progressive forces in the "Global South" was needed.

Ukrainian society has been repeating the slogan "Ukraine is Europe" for a decade. The insistency with which it is being constantly repeated makes one wonder whether those who keep proclaiming it are not trying to convince themselves of something not really evident. It is of little interest to state handbook facts, according to which the European continent stretches from the Atlantic to the Urals and the Caspian Sea. In the social reality that we live in, "Europe" stands for one of the richest regions of the world, dominating much of the rest of the planet politically and economically. There are also numerous inequalities inside the imagined "Europe." Claiming that Ukraine is a part of this prosperous and powerful bloc would be presumptuous. Hence, a reality of Ukrainian society, that it is built into global capitalist hierarchies as a periphery, cries out for materialist analysis, instead of the idealistic and sometimes racist proclamation of Ukraine being the part of "European civilization." Europe remains of course an important point of reference, as we are anyway situated in the region and Ukrainian history and current events are deeply related with the neighboring countries. But it is useful to reflect on our place in European hierarchies and to decenter our optics and look for productive comparisons or shared experiences elsewhere, in equally peripheral places, to find our common ways of challenging the existing exploitative system of global inequalities.

PT: On the situation in Ukraine, many articles are published. What are the specificities of your publications on this subject? What are the main concerns of your choice of articles? What do you say that others do not?

C: Well, we differ from foreign left-wing publications in that we are a Ukrainian media, and from Ukrainian ones in that we are one of the few left-wing media in Ukraine. As any progressive leftists would agree — it is important to give voice to the people on the ground and, hence, we are voicing our perspective and are trying to give voice to diverse groups and experiences from Ukraine. Unlike many other media from Ukraine, we, as a left media, consider the topics of current inequalities, exploitation, and paths to a more egalitarian and just society to be the most important.

PT: What place does Marxism have in your thinking?

C: This is probably a question that each member of the editorial board should answer individually. Some of us are Marxists, but not all of us, and among the journal's co-founders and former editors there were people of various views, including anarchists. However, a materialist approach to reality is what unites all the editors.

We have translated the works of many Marxist authors, such as Perry Anderson, Étienne Balibar, Tithi Bhattacharya, Hal Draper, David Harvey, Nancy Fraser, Michael Löwy, Marcel van der Linden, Nicos Poulantzas, Beverly J. Silver, Enzo Traverso, and Erik Olin Wright to name a few. At the same time, we translated anarchist authors, such as David Graeber and Peter Gelderloos, and just progressive scholars, such as Randall Collins and Pierre Bourdieu. We also pay special attention to the intellectual legacy of Roman Rosdolsky, one of the most prominent Ukrainian Marxists.

PT: You have edited the paper magazine Commons. Its last issue was in June 2019. Why did you stop?

C: It requires a lot of time and effort, and there is not much benefit from it. Though it allowed us to provide a more holistic approach to a selected topic and to engage the most active people into a leftist perspective, online publications allow us to reach out to more people and to pursue an attempt to make a more general shift in public discussion. In addition, while our issues were thematic, usually a particular topic was of interest to only a portion of the editorial board, while the rest were less involved. In the end, we are deeply appreciating that experience and some of us have a bit of nostalgic feeling toward print issues, but at some point we decided to move forward.

PT: On your website you offer books for free download (for example, Who will look after the children? Kindergartens in the context of gender inequality; A future without capitalism; Cybernetics and democratic economic governance). Do you plan to publish your own books in the future?

C: These books (some of which are rather research reports, others edited volumes) came into being as a result of a particular interest and engagement of some of

the editors leading the publication or undertaking the research. Some of them were also edited by people outside *Commons*, but with whom we share common ideas and visions.

We are currently preparing an important book on the results of the special project on Just Transition. It will be available in Ukrainian and adapted for an English-speaking audience.

PT: On your website you say "The editorial board shares egalitarian and anti-capitalist views. That is why in our publications we discuss how to change society so that there is no room for exploitation, inequality and discrimination." How is this reflected in your functioning and in your choice of articles?

C: Of course, our ideological perspective influences the choice of articles. We cannot say that we publish only authors who have the same ideological viewpoint as we do. Yes, most of our publications come from like-minded people. But we also sometimes publish pieces with which we agree, though the frame of the article is not necessarily leftist; nevertheless it should, of course, contain nothing contrary to our beliefs, like racism, elitist sentiments, misogyny, market-based approaches, and so on. The idea to construct a dialogue with peripheral experiences comes directly from our views. It is important for us to push forward the equal voice of women and give the perspective of workers. In our everyday work we are aware of the different and often unequal situations of editors and external people, with whom we cooperate. We are aware that some of us have full-time jobs to support their living. We take into account that some have care obligations, which have a significant impact on their working time and schedule.

PT: Since the start of the full-scale war on February 24, 2022, how have you been working and how has this changed your publishing policy?

C: In the first months of the invasion, we switched almost completely to an international audience, although before that we paid little attention to the English version of the site. We felt it important to engage into regional and global leftist debates about the Russian invasion, and to promote our perspective on what genuine internationalism and solidarity means in a situation like this. When the discussion about the post-war reconstruction of Ukraine started sometime in summer 2022, we considered it important to promote the idea of a just reconstruction. By the end of the previous year we had consolidated the idea of the dialogues of the peripheries, though it was under internal discussion for some months already. This makes the English-language publication continuously important for us and we are trying to translate a substantial portion of our texts and planning to do it further.

We also have built and continue building connections with different progressive media and activists from other countries and this helps to increase the variety of authors and perspectives. From a more organizational perspective, we also have to adjust a lot. The personal situations of many of our editors and authors have changed because of the full-scale invasion. Some had to relocate within Ukraine, some had to flee abroad, some went to the army, some became enforced single mothers (due to the Ukrainian government's restriction on border mobility for men). Our work in spring 2022 was a bit chaotic as the general and personal circumstances were constantly changing. Now the situation is settled to an extent, and we work together mostly using online communication. Paradoxically, the COVID-19 pandemic had prepared us for this from a technical and practical point of view.

PT: Do you have relationships with other websites in Europe or internationally?

C: We have numerous relationships with different media, mostly in Europe, but also in the US, Latin America, etc. We are members of the East European networks ELMO and cooperate with others from time to time. We have far fewer contacts with media from similarly peripheral countries, outside Eastern Europe or Latin America. But we also have some plans and ideas, which we are now working on together with other people in order to facilitate communication and cooperation worldwide.

Since the full-scale invasion began, we have seen a doubling in the number of websites that have translated, reprinted, or linked to our publications in their articles. In one year, this number has grown to almost 2,000 sites worldwide. And the number of active backlinks to our publications rose five times to more than 150,000.

Some of the media have gotten our permission and published translations of our articles. But the majority of them do it themselves. And we welcome this kind of distribution.

So our articles, especially on the Russian-Ukrainian war, which we started to publish actively in English, have started to influence the political discussion in other countries around the world.

PT: How many readers do you have? How many people visit your website?

C: We have our own stable core audience. Overall, the site is read by about 30,000 readers a month. About half of them are foreign audiences, which have doubled since the invasion began. We also spread our ideas and values through social media, using shorter and more accessible formats. In such a way we are aiming to reach younger people, creating highlights of articles in the Instagram account and on Twitter, for example.

17.05.2023
first published on *New Politics*

To the Western Left

A Letter to the Western Left from Kyiv

Taras Bilous

Translated by **Denys Gorbach**

I am writing these lines in Kyiv while it is under artillery attack.

Until the last minute, I had hoped that Russian troops wouldn't launch a full-scale invasion. Now, I can only thank those who leaked the information to the US intelligence services.

Yesterday, I spent half the day considering whether I ought to join a territorial defence unit. During the night that followed, the Ukrainian president Volodymyr Zelenskyi signed a full mobilisation order and Russian troops moved in and prepared to encircle Kyiv, which made the decision for me.

But before taking up my post, I would like to communicate to the Western Left what I think about its reaction to Russia's aggression against Ukraine.

First of all, I am thankful to those Leftists who are now picketing Russian embassies — even those who took their time to realise Russia was the aggressor in this conflict.

I am thankful to politicians who support putting pressure on Russia to stop the invasion and withdraw its troops.

And I am thankful to the delegation of British and Welsh MPs, unionists, and activists who came to support us and hear us in the days before the Russian invasion.

I am also thankful to the Ukraine Solidarity Campaign in the UK for its help over many years.

This article is about the other part of the Western Left. Those who imagined 'NATO aggression in Ukraine', and who could not see Russian aggression — like the New Orleans chapter of the Democratic Socialists of America (DSA).

Or the DSA International Committee, which published a shameful statement failing to say a single critical word against Russia (I am very thankful to US professor and activist Dan la Botz and the others for their critique of this statement).

Or those who criticised Ukraine for not implementing the Minsk Agreements and kept silent about their violations by Russia and the so-called 'People's Republics'.

Or those who exaggerated the influence of the far-Right in Ukraine, but did not notice the far-Right in the 'People's Republics' and avoided criticising Putin's conservative, nationalist and authoritarian policy. Part of the responsibility for what is happening rests with you.

This is part of the wider phenomenon in the Western 'anti-war' movement, usually called 'campism' by critics on the Left. British-Syrian author and activist Leila Al-Shaml gave it a stronger name: the "anti-imperialism of idiots". Read her wonderful 2018 essay if you haven't done so yet. I will repeat only the main thesis here: the activity of a large part of the Western 'anti-war' Left over the war in Syria had nothing to do with stopping the war. It only opposed Western interference, while ignoring, or even supporting, the engagement of Russia and Iran, to say nothing of their attitude to the 'legitimately elected' Assad regime in Syria.

"A number of anti-war organisations have justified their silence on Russian and Iranian interventions by arguing that 'the main enemy is at home,'" Al-Shaml wrote. "This excuses them from undertaking any serious power analysis to determine who the main actors driving the war actually are."

Unfortunately, we have seen the same ideological cliché repeated over Ukraine. Even after Russia recognised the independence of the 'People's Republics' earlier this week, Branko Marcetic, a writer for American Left magazine *Jacobin*, penned an article almost fully devoted to criticising the US. When it came to Putin's intentions, he

Taras Bilous is Ukrainian historian, co-editor of *Commons* journal, an activist of the *Social Movement* organization, currently serving in the Ukrainian Armed Forces.

went only as far as remarking that the Russian leader had "signal[led] less-than-benign ambitions". Seriously?

I am not a fan of NATO. I know that after the end of the Cold War, the bloc lost its defensive function and led aggressive policies. I know that NATO's eastward expansion undermined efforts directed at nuclear disarmament and forming a system of joint security. NATO tried to marginalise the role of the UN and the Organisation for Security and Co-operation in Europe, and to discredit them as 'inefficient organisations'. But we cannot bring back the past, and we have to orient ourselves on the current circumstances when seeking a way out of this situation.

How many times did the Western Left bring up the US's informal promises to the former Russian president, Mikhail Gorbachev, about NATO ("not one inch eastward"), and how many times did it mention the 1994 Budapest Memorandum that guarantees Ukraine's sovereignty? How often did the Western Left support the "legitimate security concerns" of Russia, a state that owns the world's second-largest nuclear arsenal? And how often did it recall the security concerns of Ukraine, a state that had to trade its nuclear weapons, under the pressure of the US and Russia, for a piece of paper (the Budapest Memorandum) that Putin trampled conclusively in 2014? Did it ever occur to Leftist critics of NATO that Ukraine is the main victim of the changes brought about by the NATO expansion?

Time and again, the Western Left responded to the critique of Russia by mentioning US aggression against Afghanistan, Iraq and other states. Of course, these states need to be brought into the discussion — but how, exactly?

The argument of the Left should be, that in 2003, other governments did not put enough pressure on the United States over Iraq. Not that it is necessary to exert less pressure on Russia over Ukraine now.

An obvious mistake

Imagine for a moment that, in 2003, when the US was preparing for the invasion of Iraq, Russia had behaved like the US has in recent weeks: with threats of escalation.

Now imagine what the Russian Left might have done in that situation, according to the dogma of 'our main enemy is at home'. Would it have criticised the Russian government for this 'escalation', saying that it 'should not jeopardise inter-imperialist contradictions'? It is obvious to everyone that such behaviour would have been a mistake in that case. Why was this not obvious in the case of the aggression against Ukraine?

In another *Jacobin* article from earlier this month, Marcetic went as far as saying that Fox News's Tucker Carlson was "completely right" about the "Ukrainian crisis". What Carlson had done was question "Ukraine's strategic value to the United States". Even Tariq Ali in the *New Left Review* approvingly quoted the calculation of German admiral Kay-Achim Schönbach, who said that giving Putin "respect" over Ukraine was "low cost, even no cost" given that Russia could be a useful ally against China. Are you serious? If the US and Russia could reach an agreement and start a new Cold War against China as allies, would that really be what we wanted?

Reforming the UN

I am not a fan of liberal internationalism. Socialists should criticise it. But this does not mean that we have to support the division of 'spheres of interest' between imperialist states. Instead of looking for a new balance between the two imperialisms, the Left has to struggle for a democratisation of the international security order. We need a global policy and a global system of international security. We have the latter: it is the UN. Yes, it has plenty of flaws, and it is often the object of fair criticisms. But one can criticise either to refute something or to improve it. In the case of the UN, we need the latter. We need a Leftist vision of reform and democratisation of the UN.

Of course, this does not mean that the Left should support all of the UN's decisions. But an overall reinforcement of the UN's role in the resolution of armed conflicts would allow the Left to minimise the importance of military-political alliances and reduce the number of victims. (In a previous article, I wrote how UN peacekeepers could have helped to resolve the Donbas conflict. Unfortunately, this has now lost its relevance.) After all, we also need the UN to solve the climate crisis and other global problems. The reluctance of many international Leftists to appeal to it is a terrible mistake.

After Russian troops invaded *Ukraine, Jacobin's* Europe editor David Broder wrote that the Left "should make no apologies for opposing a US military response". This was not Biden's intention anyway, as he said multiple times. But a large part of the Western Left should honestly admit that it completely fucked up in formulating its response to the "Ukrainian crisis".

My perspective

I will finish by briefly writing about myself and my perspective.

Over the past eight years, the Donbas war has been the main issue that has divided the Ukrainian Left. Each of us formed our position under the influence of personal experience and other factors. Thus, another Ukrainian Leftist would have written this article differently.

I was born in the Donbas, but in a Ukrainian-speaking and nationalist family. My father became involved in the far-Right in the 1990s, observing Ukraine's economic decay and the enrichment of the former Communist Party leadership, which he had been fighting since the mid-1980s. Of course, he has very anti-Russian, but also anti-American views. I still remember his words on 11 September 2001. As he watched the Twin Towers falling on TV, he said that those responsible were 'heroes' (he does not think so anymore — now he believes that the Americans blew them up on purpose).

When the war began in Donbas in 2014, my father joined one of the volunteer battalions, my mother fled Luhansk, and my grandfather and grandmother stayed in their village which fell under the control of the 'Luhansk People's Republic'. My grandfather condemned Ukraine's Euromaidan revolution. He supports Putin, who, he says, has "restored order in Russia". Nevertheless, we all try to keep talking to each other (though not about politics) and to help each other. I try to be sympathetic towards them. After all, my grandfather and grandmother spent their whole life working on a collective farm. My father was a construction worker. Life has not been kind to them.

The events of 2014 — revolution followed by war — pushed me in the opposite direction of most people in Ukraine. The war killed nationalism in me and pushed me to the Left. I want to fight for a better future for humanity, and not for the nation. My parents, with their post-Soviet trauma, do not understand my socialist views. My father is condescending about my 'pacifism', and we had a nasty conversation after I showed up at an anti-fascist protest with a picket sign calling for the disbanding of the far-Right Azov regiment.

When Volodymyr ZelenskyI became president of Ukraine in the spring of 2019, I hoped this could prevent the catastrophe that is unfolding now. After all, it is difficult to demonise a Russian-speaking president who won with a programme of peace for Donbas and whose jokes were popular among Ukrainians as well as Russians. Unfortunately, I was mistaken. While Zelenskyi's victory changed the attitude of many Russians towards Ukraine, this did not prevent the war.

In recent years, I have written about the peace process and about civilian victims on both sides of the Donbas war. I tried to promote dialogue. But this has all gone up in smoke now. There will be no compromise. Putin can plan whatever he wants, but even if Russia seizes Kyiv and instals its occupational government, we will resist it. The struggle will last until Russia gets out of Ukraine and pays for all the victims and all the destruction.

Hence, my last words are addressed to the Russian people: hurry up and overthrow the Putin regime. It is in your interests as well as ours.

25.02.2022

Ten Terrible Leftist Arguments against Ukrainian Resistance

Oksana Dutchak

Discussions with some on the (mostly) western left can be extremely hard. Some of their positions are disheartening to hear. Others seem hypocritical or cynical. There are, in my opinion, certain positions that are far from left principles. These points are not always expressed directly, so I want to briefly dig into some hidden messages underlying positions held by many on the left.

Disclaimer #1: I want to stress that there are also a lot of leftists who take the position of solidarity and will have zero to do with these claims. However, here I am not writing about them.

Disclaimer #2: It really matters how some of these messages are voiced as this draws the line between, on the one hand, points of concern and discussion, and on the other — the central pillar of one's predetermined and unconditional political stand against Ukrainian resistance. This text is about the second case. I won't discuss nuances here. This is a polemic opinion, not an analytical article.

Disclaimer #3: I'm frustrated, angry and, hence, often sarcastic here. And yes, I have the right to be so. And yes, I use this piece to channel my frustration and anger.

***

1. "If another country attacks my country, I would just flee"

Well, I've done the same because I have two children. The unvoiced full version of the claim: *"In a hypothetical situation which is highly unlikely, but which I still project*

on you, I will not support any collective resistance to the invasion and because of this projection I oppose Ukrainian resistance". This claim is mostly expressed by people from countries without any modern history of being subject to nor under the threat of imperial domination. But we are not in an abstract war here or in any version of your projections. It is a very concrete imperial invasion backed by the rhetoric of total submission. Sometimes it also reaches the level of genocidal rhetoric. A Marxist should have a triple facepalm hearing that the war against imperial oppression is not worth fighting. Of course, if something like this ever happens to you, you can choose the option of not resisting and I would never judge you as long as you don't use your individual choice to condemn the collective defensive struggle of others in a totally and structurally different reality.

2. "I would never fight for my government"

The unvoiced full version of the claim: *"1) Ukrainians are fighting for their government, 2) I think so for no reason and I either have not checked this claim with Ukrainians or 3) I don't think Ukrainians' opinion should be taken into account anyway".* Well, quite obvious — this war has nothing to do with our shitty (like many others) government. Check the fucking opinion polls which some leftists like so much when they support their point and immediately forget about when they undermine it. If this war ever had anything to do with the Ukrainian government, the government stopped being relevant the second Russian propaganda started to talk about "the solution of the Ukrainian question" and "denazification" of the population, en masse.

Oksana Dutchak is a member of the editorial team of the *Commons*, PhD in social sciences. Research interests: protests, workers' protests, gender inequality, care labor, Marxism, Marxist feminism.

The second part of this unvoiced claim is tied to a total detachment from material reality and disregard of it — a very materialist approach, indeed. The third part of the claim has, of course, nothing to do with left principles and is, unfortunately, like many other points, an obvious manifestation of west-centric, patronizing or arrogant "leftism".

Probably the most stunning variations of this position are "analyses" of the war with numerous factual mistakes by people who know almost nothing about the region and manifestos "against the war" without a single Ukrainian signature. Being a left academic "superstar" is a guarantee many people will still take your text seriously, despite the desperately lamenting material reality and human bodies buried under its rubble.

3. "Our government supports Ukraine and I can never take the side of my government"

The unvoiced full message of this claim is: *"In fact I do support my government in many instances, but in such a way I justify my stand against supporting Ukrainian resistance and/or rely on identity politics instead of materialist principles to make my life conformist and simple"*. Of course, these people support their governments on some occasions and criticize and oppose it on others. Reality is complicated, you know. Sometimes even shitty governments do the right thing, especially under pressure from popular progressive struggle. It is like opposing migrants and refugees, which the government decided to "let in", because it was the government's position. (I know, I know that some do this under the slogans that "they will take our workers' jobs"). An illusory principled opposition to one's own government is simply used, again, as a justification of opposition to Ukrainian resistance. Seriously supporting this claim means relying on identity politics based on blind universalization instead of an analysis of the material reality facing Ukraine.

4. "Ukrainian and Russian workers, instead of fighting with each other, should turn their guns against their own governments"

The unvoiced message here is: *"I prefer to do nothing in this situation where there is no direct or indirect threat to my life, I'm opposing Ukrainian resistance and I want to find a nice, leftist-sounding justification"*. Yeah, we should better pretend to be stones and wait for a global proletarian revolution. Well, I'm afraid at some moment such people will even claim there is no need to wage any social struggle until the global revolution (I know, I know that some almost do). This position, however, is (often) the position of a privileged individual which hides ideological egoism behind nice rhetoric. It is also a product of the years-long decline in left mobilization and the global system's many reactionary turns. A very good and universal shit, if somebody wants to do the shitbath, I recommend this one.

5. "Who benefits from this war?"

The unvoiced message is: *"I know that some parts of the elite capitalist class benefit almost from anything in this world, because it is how the system works, but I still use this question (which is not really a question) to express my opposition to Ukrainian struggle for self-determination"*. Opposing such a struggle because western elites benefit from it is like opposing industrial action because a capitalist competitor benefits from it. Another variation of this claim is part of the NATO weapon discussion (though, of course, I know the discussion is more complicated). Sorry, but we live in a world without a progressive state of the size required to provide material support to a struggle of this scale and benefit from its victory. Unless you consider other imperial powers like China to be progressive.

This shithole is also a good one to go for as it is a deep one and can contain many variations. Most of the discussion about the "spheres of influence" falls into this shithole too in one way or another. Taking this position seriously means taking the side of the reactionary status quo we have been living in for decades. It also often goes together with denial, devaluation or even favoritism of Russian (or any non-western) imperialism. Sometimes it also hides all the other thoughts, like supporting any cannibalistic regime against western imperialism. On the part of some leftists from the Global South it can hide the lust for revenge — this lust, though being far more understandable than the conformist identity politics of western observers, contains a nasty disregard of Ukrainian people on whose expense the revenge against western imperialism must be waged.

6. "What about the far right on the Ukrainian side?"

The hidden claim here is: *"I use the far right problem as a fig leaf to hide my opposition to Ukrainian resistance"*. Yeah, there are far right groups in Ukraine — like in many other countries — and yes, they have weapons now because, surprise, we are at war. But those who voice this claim mostly don't care about the far right on the side of the Russian army or the general scary far-right path of Russian politics with respective implications for its internal and foreign "affairs" (like, yeah, the row of wars). They don't care that some left political scientists from Russia now call their regime a post-fascist one. They don't know about how big is the participation of far right in Ukrainian resistance, they don't care about participation of other ideological groups and the general scale of the resistance, they don't know how the empty signifier of "nazi" is used by Russian propaganda to dehumanize whoever they want. It is just a fig leaf which, thanks to Russian propaganda and some other factors, has grown into a colossus.

7. "Russia and Ukraine should negotiate. Upgraded version: here are our propositions for a peace deal"

This claim has many hidden variations, which depends on the propositions of a peace deal those people voice. Depending on these propositions, the unvoiced message can be: *"1) Ukraine should capitulate or 2) we are detached*

from reality and think our relatively reasonable propositions of a peace deal are realistic now". The first option is the same good old "peace by any means": the propositions basically presuppose that Ukraine should give up on newly captured territories and follow almost all the absurd political demands of Russia, giving up the country's independence and people's self-determination. Very leftist, indeed. In the second option the proposed peace deal is close to the one that was on the negotiation table in spring, when the full scale invasion just started. One of the main points of the proposed peace deal is that the Russian army must retreat from the newly captured territories — to the border on the 23rd of February. This point makes the whole proposition useless at this moment of time and the proposers cannot give a reasonable answer to the questions why should the Putin regime do that on this stage, who and how can "persuade" it to do this.

There is also the uglier version of the unvoiced message: *"we are sane, knowing our relatively reasonable propositions are unrealistic at the moment, but we still voice them to show that those stupid Ukrainians don't want to negotiate"*.

8. "The West should stop supporting Ukraine because it may escalate into a nuclear war"

The hidden message: *"any nuclear country can do whatever she wants because we are afraid"*. You know, I'm also afraid of nuclear war. But keeping to this position is supporting the reactionary status quo and facilitating imperialist politics. And what is missing from this discussion are disastrous consequences of Russia's attack for the global movement for nuclear disarmament. Now I can hardly imagine why any country would give up its nuclear arsenal voluntarily being afraid to follow the "destiny" of Ukraine (google "Budapest Memorandum"). And this is not the West to blame here.

9. "We won't even talk to you because you are for weapons"

The hidden message: *"we don't care about the material reality of this war and sorry-not-sorry that you were unlucky enough to be attacked by a non-western imperial country, just do not make uncomfortable interventions into our imagined monolithic unipolar and west-centric internationalism"*. This is, of course, an intersection of many of the previous claims but I've decided to put it separately because this is a brilliant manifestation we, Ukrainian leftists, hear sometimes and wonder about solidarity, internationalism, attention to the structures of power inequality, anti-imperialism and all that, you know, important things, thrown into the trash at broad daylight in front of our eyes.

10. "Good Russian resistance vs. bad/inconvenient/non-existing Ukrainian resistance"

And last, but not least – actually this one triggers me the most. This shit triggers me immensely and brings some irrational emotions I'm ashamed of. There is no hidden message here. One of the extreme examples is when the left meeting is addressed by a Russian anti-war activist and everybody listens, but when the same meeting is addressed by a Ukrainian left with basically the same messages, some people demonstratively leave the room and boo. The Ukrainian leftists can be questioned as if they have no right to participate in a discussion about this war if no Russian war-opposer is involved – even if just in a few days they participate in another discussion with Russian anti-war representatives. How dare the Ukrainian leftists speak about Russian invasion without the Russian leftists, right?

These are only extreme examples, but there is a sea of moderate variations: supporting and admiring Russian anti-war resistance and being numb about the Ukrainian one. Spreading some messages of the Russian anti-war movement and ignoring the messages of Ukrainian leftist. Pretending Ukrainian resistance does not exist. Writing about brave and strong Russian war-opposers and, at the same time, describing Ukrainians only as civilian losses, refugees, poor victims.

Russian anti-war resistance often voices similar claims and supports the Ukrainian left in relation to the war: they demand weapons for Ukrainian resistance, they want Russia to lose! Puzzling, that this similarity doesn't matter, right? However, the explanation is simple. Russian anti-war resistance is comfortable, it corresponds to many hidden claims and messages. They are against their government. They don't have guns in their hands. In the end, they are brave and worth listening to, unlike poor/stubborn/nationalistic/militaristic – in other words, inconvenient – Ukrainian left, who refuse to be comfortable victims. You know why this difference between Ukrainian left resistance and Russian anti-war resistance appeared? Because it is not Russia which is under imperial attack, and it is not the Russian opposition which is waging a defensive war for self-determination.

***

I know some hidden claims and messages are missing. Some of them are so obviously bullshit to discuss, like "but the USA has done much worse", "socialist Russia", "nazi regime in Kiev", "14000 civilians, killed by Ukrainian government", "don't be so emotional", "there is nothing good to defend in Ukraine" (yes, this is a real one!). There are also some points which are too painful for me to discuss now.

I know that internationalism and practical solidarity are not falling apart for the first time. But you cannot even approach (again) its reconstruction, ignoring what is behind the hidden messages: idealistic delusions, structures of political power inequality, reactionary currents and all the other shit which allows so many to look away in the face of Russian imperialism and Ukrainian struggle for self-determination.

20.07.2022

The Right to Resist: A Feminist Manifesto

The Feminist Initiative Group

We, feminists from Ukraine, call on feminists around the world to stand in solidarity with the resistance movement of the Ukrainian people against the predatory, imperialist war unleashed by the Russian Federation. War narratives often portray women* as victims. However, in reality, women* also play a key role in resistance movements, both at the frontline and on the home front: from Algeria to Vietnam, from Syria to Palestine, from Kurdistan to Ukraine.

The authors of the Feminist Resistance Against War manifesto deny Ukrainian women* this right to resistance, which constitutes a basic act of self-defense of the oppressed. In contrast, we view feminist solidarity as a political practice which must listen to the voices of those directly affected by imperialist aggression. Feminist solidarity must defend women's* right to independently determine their needs, political goals, and strategies for achieving them. Ukrainian feminists were struggling against systemic discrimination, patriarchy, racism, and capitalist exploitation long before the present moment. We conducted and will continue to conduct this struggle both during war and in peacetime. However, the Russian invasion is forcing us to focus on the general defense effort of Ukrainian society: the fight for survival, for basic rights and freedoms, for political self-determination. We call for an informed assessment of a specific situation instead of abstract geopolitical analysis which ignores the historical, social and political context. Abstract pacifism which condemns all sides taking part in the war leads to irresponsible solutions in practice. We insist on the essential difference between violence as a means of oppression and as a legitimate means of self-defense.

The Russian aggression undermines the achievements of Ukrainian feminists in the struggle against political and social oppression. In the occupied territories, the Russian army uses mass rape and other forms of gender-based violence as a military strategy. The establishment of the Russian regime in these territories poses the threat of criminalizing LGBTIQ+ people and decriminalizing domestic violence. Throughout Ukraine, the problem of domestic violence is becoming more acute. Vast destruction of civilian infrastructure, threats to the environmental, inflation, shortages, and population displacement endanger social reproduction. The war intensifies gendered division of labor, further shifting the work of social reproduction — in especially difficult and precarious conditions — onto women. Rising unemployment and the neoliberal government's attack on labor rights continue to exacerbate social problems. Fleeing from the war, many women* are forced to leave the country, and find themselves in a vulnerable position due to barriers to housing, social infrastructure, stable income, and medical services (including contraception and abortion). They are also at risk of getting trapped into sex trafficking.

We call on feminists from around the world to support our struggle. We demand:

• the right to self-determination, protection of life and fundamental freedoms, and the right to self-defense (including armed) for the Ukrainian people — as well as for other peoples facing imperialist aggression;
• a just peace, based on the self-determination of the Ukrainian people, both in the territories controlled by Ukraine and its temporarily occupied territories, in which the interests of workers, women, LGBTIQ+ people, ethnic minorities and other oppressed and discriminated groups will be taken into account;

- international justice for war crimes and crimes against humanity during the imperialist wars of the Russian Federation and other countries;
- effective security guarantees for Ukraine and effective mechanisms to prevent further wars, aggression, escalation of conflicts in the region and in the world;
- freedom of movement, protection and social security for all refugees and internally displaced persons irrespective of origin;
- protection and expansion of labor rights, opposition to exploitation and super exploitation, and democratization of industrial relations;
- prioritization of the sphere of social reproduction (kindergartens, schools, medical institutions, social support, etc.) in the reconstruction of Ukraine after the war;
- cancellation of Ukraine's foreign debt (and that of other countries of the global periphery) for post-war reconstruction and prevention of further austerity policies;
- protection against gender-based violence and guaranteed effective implementation of the Istanbul Convention;
- respect for the rights and empowerment of LGBTIQ+ people, national minorities, people with disabilities and other discriminated groups;
- implementation of the reproductive rights of girls and women, including the universal rights to sex education, medical services, medicine, contraception, and abortion;
- guaranteed visibility for and recognition of women's active role in the anti-imperialist struggle;
- inclusion of women in all social processes and decision-making, both during war and in peacetime, on equal terms with men;

Today, Russian imperialism threatens the existence of Ukrainian society and affects the entire world. Our common fight against it requires shared principles and global support. We call for feminist solidarity and action to protect human lives as well as rights, social justice, freedom, and security.

We stand for the right to resist.

If Ukrainian society lays down its arms, there will be no Ukrainian society.

If Russia lays down its arms, the war will end.

Sign the manifesto on our website: https://commons.com.ua/en/right-resist-feminist-manifesto/

07.07.2022

The War in Ukraine, International Security, and the Left

Taras Bilous

Translated from Ukrainian by **Yuril Hlazov**

"The Russian invasion of Ukraine has no justification, but NATO..." It is difficult to describe the emotions I and other Ukrainian socialists feel about this "but" in the statements and articles of many Western leftists. Unfortunately, it is often followed by attempts to present the Russian invasion as a defensive reaction to the "aggressive expansion of NATO" and thus to shift much of the responsibility for the invasion to the West.

One example of this is Susan Watkins' editorial article in *New Left Review*. In it, the author calls the Russian invasion of a country that is not now and is unlikely to ever become a member of NATO a "war of Russia against NATO," effectively denying Ukraine's subjectivity. In addition, Watkins argues that Biden "could no doubt have prevented an invasion had he been willing to negotiate a serious agreement on military frontiers."

Such a position has been met with criticism from Eastern European leftist authors, in particular Jan Smolenskl and Jan Dutkiewicz. They pointed out that the Eastern European states joined NATO voluntarily, with the support of the majority of their populations, and did so given their own concerns, usually ignored by critics of NATO enlargement.

Since these issues are often a stumbling block in leftist discussions of the war in Ukraine, let's examine them in more detail — especially since, in my view, they are also important for shaping leftist strategy on international security issues.

Finlandization

Could this war have been avoided by agreeing that Ukraine would not join NATO? Any serious answer to this question must take into account the fact that in the run-up to the war, the Kremlin demanded far more than that. In particular, the draft treaty between Russia and the United States, published by the Russian Foreign Ministry on December 17, included a clause stating that the US would not develop bilateral military cooperation with states that were formerly part of the Soviet Union and not members of NATO (Article 4) — Ukraine, Georgia, and Moldova.

Some readers may assume that this clause appeared in the draft treaties so that later there would be something to concede during negotiations, but there are good reasons to doubt it. Shortly before the draft treaties appeared, Dmitrl Trenin, director of the Carnegie Moscow Center, and Alexander Baunov, a fellow at the same center, wrote that for Moscow's elites, close military cooperation between Ukraine and the United States had become as unacceptable as Ukraine's accession to NATO.

Therefore, although the media often reduced Russia's demands to Ukraine's neutrality, they were in fact more serious. The European neutral states, in particular Switzerland, Austria, Sweden, and Finland, are not prevented by their status from developing cooperation with the United States in the field of armaments. All these states also take part in NATO's Partnership for Peace program. Military cooperation between Ukraine and the United States also began when Ukraine declared its non-bloc status. Ukraine and the USA signed a treaty on military cooperation in 1993, Ukraine and the USA have been organizing the international military exercise Sea Breeze since 1997, and Russia took part in it in 1998.

After 2014, military cooperation with the United States and NATO was an important factor in the modernization of the Ukrainian army. Without it, Ukrainian resistance to Russian invasion would have been significantly less effective. Had this cooperation ceased at Russia's request, Ukraine would have been less secure, and therefore the Ukrainian government might have been forced to comply with other Russian demands. In this regard, the term

Taras Bilous is Ukrainian historian, co-editor of *Commons* journal, an activist of the *Social Movement* organization, currently serving in the Ukrainian Armed Forces.

"Finlandization," used by many authors, better describes the essence of Russian demands. During the Cold War, Finland not only did not join NATO, but also took into account numerous "wishes" of the Soviet leadership, in particular, it rejected the Marshall Plan and extradited all fugitives from the USSR. (In addition, the Finno-Soviet Treaty of 1948 provided for military cooperation between Finland and the USSR in the event of an attack on the USSR through Finland.)

Finland pursued this policy after its defeat in the war, in which it was allied with Nazi Germany. Realizing that the Soviet leadership could turn Finland into another satellite if it so desired, agreeing to certain restrictions in exchange for maintaining its political system and sovereignty was a rational solution for the Finns. At the same time, Ukraine was not in such a predicament before the current war, and most did not agree to Russian demands.

Here the difference between the original "Finlandization" and the situation on the eve of the Russian invasion of Ukraine is obvious. The Finnish policy of neutrality and consideration of Soviet interests was based on agreements between Finland and the USSR, while in Ukraine the Kremlin wanted to negotiate with the United States and NATO. At the time, the Kremlin had apparently lost hope that it would be possible to force the Ukrainian authorities to comply with Russian demands, or that pro-Russian forces would come to power in Ukraine. Therefore, the Kremlin decided, against the wishes of Ukraine's people, to negotiate the future of Ukraine with those whom it viewed as the "masters" of that power.

It should be noted that the Kremlin may have needed the draft treaties not as a last attempt to negotiate, but to legitimize its invasion. We don't know exactly when Putin made the decision to invade, and we will only be able to say for sure once the Kremlin archives are opened. But we can assess the information that is available to us. The essence of the Russian proposals was practically a division of Europe into spheres of influence between Russia and the US. I do not know if Susan Watkins understands this, but that is what she actually supported in her *New Left Review* essay, writing "In calling for a stable settlement of military borders, the Kremlin has a good case."

The Cuban Missile Crisis

Imagine: A nationalist revolution takes place in a country near an imperialist state that regards the territory as its sphere of influence. The imperialist state attempts to prevent the ultimate loss of influence over the politics of the first country using brute force and in league with opponents of the revolution. A post-revolutionary government regards an alliance with a rival superpower as a guarantee of security. The threat of nuclear war arises. This is a story not only about Ukraine, but also about another country with which many authors, including the aforementioned Dmitri Trenin, have compared Ukraine — Cuba.

Of course, there are many differences between those two cases. The class and ideological nature of the revolutions and superpowers were very different. But as far as international security is concerned, these differences are not decisive. The Cuban Missile Crisis is indeed a good analogy for Russian aggression against Ukraine, so let's look at it a little more closely.

The Cuban Missile Crisis arose from the deployment of Soviet nuclear missiles in Cuba and ended with their dismantling in exchange for US guarantees of non-aggression against Cuba and the withdrawal of American missiles from Turkey. Did military cooperation between Cuba and the USSR cease after that? No. Were Soviet troops (which the Cuban government viewed as a guarantee of its security) withdrawn from Cuba? No.

In Ukraine, on the other hand, there are no US missiles with nuclear warheads. Even participation in NATO does not necessarily imply the deployment of missiles — in this regard, the example of Norway, which was the only NATO country that shared a border with the USSR during the Cold War and therefore was wary of placing missiles on its territory, is quite telling.

Moreover, the US, while rejecting Russia's opposition to NATO's enlargement, has at the same time offered new arms control arrangements. According to Alexel Arbatov, a member of the Russian Academy of Sciences and a leading Russian expert on security and disarmament issues, until recently these proposals were put forward by Russia as well and were of serious interest in terms of easing tensions and strengthening European security. However, this time, the Russian leadership dismissed them as "secondary."

U.S. President John f. Kennedy gave guarantees of non-aggression against Cuba and agreed to remove American missiles from Turkey. In this way, he showed that his primary concern in this case was security. Russian President Vladimir Putin, on the other hand, rejected the US offer and went to war. In doing so, he showed that his primary concern was not security, but his desire for the return of Ukraine to Russian control, or at least the conquest of new Ukrainian territories. Indeed, the caution Western states have shown toward Russia even after the full-scale invasion began shows the hollowness of Russian security concerns. Russia has the best security guarantee — nuclear weapons. The Kremlin itself never tires of reminding us of this.

With regard to Ukraine, what if the US had made big concessions to Russia? What would they be? In the run-up to the invasion, there were numerous statements that Ukraine's accession to NATO was not on the agenda. The most outspoken was former NATO Secretary General Jaap de Hoop Scheffer: "Everyone, including Putin, knows that Ukraine will not become a NATO member in the foreseeable and unforeseeable future. It's already a buffer country. It's something you'll never hear NATO Secretary-General Jens Stoltenberg say; his position won't allow it. But I can say that now." Nevertheless, the Kremlin demanded a guarantee. Deputy Foreign Minister Sergel Ryabkov first responded to the idea of a temporary moratorium on NATO expansion by saying that it was unacceptable for Russia, and Putin himself spoke critically about it a few days before the invasion.

Most likely, the Kremlin would only have been satisfied with the complete fulfillment of its demands. But what would that mean for Ukraine? On the eve of the invasion, things were not going well for Volodymyr Zelenskyy, now a political superstar. His popularity ratings were falling, while those of his main rival, former President Petro Poroshenko, were rising. US agreement to Russia's demands would have greatly exacerbated the situation. And if the Ukrainian government, having lost US support, had met any of the Kremlin's demands, it would have been guaranteed to lead to a political crisis and an escalation of violence. It is quite possible that this would have created better conditions for the invasion of Russian troops as "peacekeepers." In this case, Ukrainian realities would have been much worse than they are now.

I am not claiming that in the last months before the invasion, the West and/or Ukraine could not have prevented war. But a serious examination of this possibility requires deeper analysis and access to the Kremlin archives. I think this will be an interesting question for future historians. In the meantime, those Western leftists, so eager to criticize the US for what Russia did, should refrain from claiming that Washington should have simply complied with Russian demands. After all, it could very easily have been the decision of one man — Vladimir Putin — to prevent the war. All he had to do was not give the order to start the invasion.

NATO expansion

Fortunately, on the question of NATO expansion historians have already provided a convincing answer. One of the best analyses published so far is Mary Elise Sarotte's book *Not One Inch: America, Russia, and the Making of Post-Cold War Stalemate*. Sarotte does a good job of showing that NATO's open-door policy has indeed undermined US-Russian cooperation on arms control and the formation of a broader international security system. NATO expansion gave trump cards to Russian revanchists and hawks and buried the political prospects of liberals who advocated closer cooperation with the West, like Foreign Minister Andrel Kozyrev.

In this sense, the growth of NATO did create favorable conditions for the outbreak of war. But *how* and *why* it happened is also important. Tony Wood, in an article in the same *New Left Review*, writes that the "emergence of an increasingly assertive and militarized Russian nationalism is inextricable from that process [NATO expansion], because it was in large part propelled and reinforced by it." But what Wood fails to ask is why NATO expansion has caused such a reaction. In my opinion, the answer can easily be found in Sarotte's book, to which Wood repeatedly refers.

Was it a reaction to the fact that legitimate Russian *security concerns* were neglected, as many authors have claimed? I don't think so. Seriously, how could the accession of the Czech Republic and Hungary to NATO create a threatening situation for Russia? It's enough to look at the map to give the obvious answer: no way. Then why was their accession to NATO perceived negatively in the Kremlin? Because they recently belonged to the Soviet zone of influence. And also because their accession was part of the formation of a new international order in which Russia no longer had the status of a superpower equal to the United States.

It was the pain of a lost empire that provoked revanchist sentiments. In Sarotte's book this is repeatedly seen as, for example, when Yeltsin demanded special status for Russia under the Partnership for Peace (PfP) program, on the grounds that Russia was a *"great country with a great army and nuclear weapons"* (p. 190). And, Eastern Europeans, after all, could observe these emotions of the Russians with their own eyes. Therefore, instead of talking about the emergence of Russian nationalism, as Tony Wood does, in my opinion it is more appropriate to talk about the transformation of Russian great-power chauvinism as a reaction to NATO's growth. When it became clear that Russia would not occupy as privileged a position in the new international order as Russian elites wanted, there was a growing desire among them to reconsider this order.

Sarotte's book also shows that, up to a certain point, the US tried to accommodate Russian sentiments so as not to obstruct the formation of a more secure international order. In particular, this manifested itself in the PfP program, which was designed to ensure that accessions to NATO would not happen too quickly, but would develop into something more. And characteristically, in President Bill Clinton's words, "Ukraine is the linchpin of the whole [PfP] idea" (p. 188). In the 1990s, it was obvious to everyone that Ukraine could not join NATO. Ukraine's accession to NATO was a red line for Moscow primarily because of the same great-power chauvinism, because of the special role Ukraine plays in Russian national mythology.

According to Sarotte, it was through Ukraine that Eastern European governments who wanted their countries to join NATO agreed to participate in the PfP as a compromise. But events in Russia, such as Yeltsin's anti-parliamentary coup in 1993 and the war in Chechnya, increasingly pushed Eastern European states to pressure the US to allow them to join NATO. They managed to get Article 5 extended to them to shield themselves from possible armed aggression from Russia. But the result was a new dividing line in Europe that separated Ukraine from its Western neighbours. Countries that were less threatened by Russian aggression became better protected, while Ukraine, for which the threat was greater, found itself in a "grey zone." This is why in December 1994, after the publication of the communiqué on NATO's open-door policy, Kyiv became nervous, while Moscow was furious (p. 201).

Another negative consequence of NATO enlargement was that the process of transforming the CSCE/OSCE, a conference for East-West dialogue created in 1970 into an international organization was never actually completed. The US decision to make NATO the bedrock of security in Europe has made the strengthening of the OSCE irrelevant. Had NATO's open-door policy started at least a few years later, it would have provided an opportunity to turn the OSCE into a more effective organization.

After the start of the full-scale Russian invasion of Ukraine, the OSCE became a completely irrelevant and most likely dead organization. But this should not prevent us from seeing alternatives to the development of the international security system. The OSCE Special Monitoring Mission had played an important role in resolving the war in Donbas. But its influence could have been much greater if its mandate had been expanded. Ukraine constantly demanded this, but thanks to consensus decision-making in the OSCE, Russia constantly blocked this decision. Thus, the Kremlin sabotaged the implementation of point 4 of the Minsk Protocol, which provided for monitoring by the OSCE mission of the *entire* section of the Ukrainian-Russian border in the combat zone (and not just at the two border checkpoints that Russia allowed until the fall 2021).

NATO and the CSTO

Before turning to the results, let's look some more at attitudes toward military alliances. It might help to compare NATO to its Russian counterpart, the CSTO (Collective Security Treaty Organization established in 1992).

First, it is possible to argue that NATO is a contradictory phenomenon, which on the one hand serves as a cover for US imperialism, and on the other hand, is an instrument of protection for many smaller countries. In the same way, the CSTO is a cover for Russian imperialism and was recently used to suppress a popular uprising in Kazakhstan, but serves as protection for a relatively democratic Armenia. Acknowledging this fact does not make you a fan of either American or Russian imperialism.

Second, Susan Watkins writes that NATO proved "dispensable" to invade Iraq, but she does not say that this was the case because of French and German resistance. It is also telling that Kazakhstan refused to send its troops to Ukraine, even though the invasion began a month and a half after the Kremlin helped suppress the uprising in Kazakhstan. But just as this was not an insurmountable obstacle for the United States — it created a Multi-National Force, bypassing NATO — so for Russia, Kazakhstan's refusal did not prevent it from launching the invasion of Ukraine. It should not be forgotten that the key problem in both cases is imperialism (American or Russian), not NATO and the CSTO.

Third, we should stop identifying all military actions of member countries of military alliances with the actions of these military alliances. It is not NATO as an organization that is now conducting a military operation in northern Syria, it is Turkey. And the problem here is Turkish hostility to the Kurds, not NATO. Likewise, if Turkey attacks Greece, it is not NATO attacking one of its members. Also, it is not the CSTO that is now at war against Ukraine, but Russia with the help of Belarus. Fortunately, Kazakhstan and Armenia are not involved in the war.

In addition, one should not identify NATO and "the West" as Susan Watkins did in her statement "NATO won the Cold War without firing a single shot." But it wasn't NATO that won the Cold War, it was the West that fired many shots. NATO is only one of the tools. It is not surprising that a group of states, some of which had an aggressive neo-colonial policy, also had among their many instruments a defensive alliance, whose functions changed only after this group of states won the Cold War.

Fourthly, the US and Russia can do without NATO and the CSTO for their imperialist policies, but there is no defense alternative for the Eastern European states and Armenia yet. And if you cannot offer an alternative to the people of countries that seek protection in such structures, it is better not to urge them to give up such protection.

An outline of a leftist strategy for international security

The decisions made in the 1990s–2000s have already become history, and the past cannot be brought back. Focusing on these mistakes now is the same as criticizing the Treaty of Versailles in 1939, when it had already lost relevance. What are needed now are concrete solutions that can hasten Russia's defeat and make today's world a safer place. On the other hand, as with the Treaty of Versailles, old mistakes can provide lessons for shaping postwar policy.

Did the expansion of NATO have an impact on the outbreak of this war? Yes. But there are very different ways of talking about this. When leftists and "realists" say that NATO expansion "provoked" Russia, they are thereby saying that to some extent the Russian invasion was at least partially justified, even if they deny it. Watkins does the same, arguing that the Russian invasion "was not unprovoked." It is the same as saying that the Cuban Revolution and the cooperation of Fidel Castro's government with the USSR provoked the United States. Of course, it is not a problem for "realists" to say so, but who on the Left would justify the aggressive US policy towards Cuba in this way?

The fact that the Cuban Revolution was more progressive than the Ukrainian Maidan is no excuse for such a double standard. If any imperialist state saw a revolution in its sphere of influence as a threat to itself and a "bad example" for other countries in its sphere, socialists should not use the fact that this revolution was supported by a rival superpower to condemn the revolution. It should also be noted that this applies not only to the Maidan of 2013–2014, but also to Ukraine's Orange Revolution of 2004. It was after the latter event, a few years before the NATO Bucharest Summit, whose declaration proclaimed that Georgia and Ukraine "will become members of NATO," that there was a noticeable landslide in Russian politics, indicating that the Russian elite viewed the events in Ukraine as a threat to itself.

The comparison with Cuba also tells us that we must treat different concerns differently. The deployment of nuclear missiles near a country's borders and the entry of a neighboring country into a military bloc or military cooperation with a rival state are of a different order. We should support and call for mutual restrictions on the deployment of nuclear weapons (and for global nuclear disarmament in general). But sometimes the only real alternative to military cooperation with one imperialist state against another is the total subjugation by an aggressive imperial power. Privileged inhabitants of Western countries, who do not have to worry that their country might be conquered by Russia, have no moral right to criticize those who seek protection in cooperation with those Western states. And if one criticizes any military cooperation, then criticism should not turn into support for the division of Europe or the world into spheres of influence.

Does this mean that the Left should have supported NATO expansion? No. Jan Smolenskl and Jan Dutkiewicz argued that an intellectually honest critique of NATO expansion would lead to a critique of Eastern European politicians and voters who have embraced the ideals of democracy and national self-determination. But it did not. Eastern European democracies had the sovereign right to make the choice they considered best for their security. But a country's entry into an international organization depends on the decision of both sides. And the US had to make a choice that would better ensure the security of not only those states that joined NATO, but also those that were not joining NATO. The addition of countries to NATO may have increased their security, while harming Ukraine's. From this perspective, the rapid transition to NATO's open-door policy was wrong.

As Mary Sarotte and Ukrainian historian Serhil Plokhy pointed out in a joint article, in the 1990s the US had a much better and much less costly chance to solve the security issue for Ukraine than it did. First, they could have prioritized the development of the Partnership for Peace program over the rapid expansion of NATO. Second, they could have given Ukraine effective security guarantees in the 1994 Budapest Memorandum. Ukraine demanded this at the time, but under general pressure from the United States and Russia, the Ukrainian government was then forced to agree to a worthless piece of paper. Not giving such guarantees in exchange for nuclear weapons was a terrible mistake that, in the long run, dealt an even greater blow to nuclear disarmament than NATO expansion.

However, that was more about the past. What conclusions can be drawn for the Left's approach to international security for the future? For the Western European Left of recent decades, if there was any alternative to NATO, it was the idea of a common international security system that would encompass "West" and "East" after the end of the Cold War. But if it made sense in the 1990s, it already looked unrealistic after 2008 and more so after 2014. For some reason, however, these leftists stubbornly ignored the fact that Russia, which in the early 1990s advocated an enhanced role for OSCE, subsequently became the main opponent of OSCE reform and strengthening. Another part of the European Left, particularly the Polish left-wing alliance Lewica, proposes a European security system as an alternative to NATO — a common army, a missile defense shield, an energy policy, etc. Such a system would help EU members but not those outside the EU. On the contrary, this project carries with it threats of "Fortress Europe" (the same could be said of the previous idea). Therefore, priority must be given to a global security system.

In the recent Athens Declaration, Jeremy Corbin, Yanis Varoufakis, and Ece Temelkuran said that "lasting peace can be achieved only by replacing all military blocs with an inclusive international security framework." It's difficult to disagree with this, but they didn't offer ways to create such a framework. At the same time, there is already a system that fits their description, although it performs its functions inefficiently: it is the UN. I know that many are skeptical of the idea of the United Nations. But so far, I have not seen any of the critics suggest a better alternative. And instead of looking for excuses for inaction, we should look for possible ways to push through changes. What is more utopian — to reform the UN, or to create from scratch a similar system that would unite the countries of the Global South and the Global North, but would be more effective?

Unfortunately, even after Zelenskyy's statement at the Security Council meeting about the need for UN reform, the only response I have seen in the left-wing media is an explanation of why this is impossible. But this article by Jon Schwarz is revealing for what it never mentions: the "Uniting for Peace" resolution as an alternative to Security Council unanimity. This resolution shows that reform is not so impossible. If the Council really cannot be reformed, its role must be marginalized. In fact, while I was writing this article, a step was taken in this direction: The General Assembly, at the initiative of Liechtenstein, adopted a resolution that provides for an emergency session of the General Assembly when a member of the Security Council uses its right of veto.

We have the prospect of an escalating confrontation between the US and China ahead of us. And in this conflict, the international Left must not repeat the mistakes many of them have made against Russia. China may not mind sharing spheres of influence with the US, but this is not something the Left should support. Instead of worrying about considering China's interests, as many leftists have worried about considering Russia's interests, we should think about how to protect small states from domination by all imperialist states. In particular, the international Left should be thinking about how to protect Taiwan without allowing war, not about how to force Taiwan into submission to the PRC. (The fact that Taiwan is not a member of the UN is a problem to be solved, not a reason not to defend Taiwan.)

Some leftist authors have pointed out that the population of states that abstained during the UN General Assembly vote on Russian aggression against Ukraine combined is nearly half the world's population. But to suggest that this represents the position of half of humanity is to ignore Chinese imperialism and the Indian far-right government. In my view, more important was Barbara Crossette's observation that small states, in particular India's neighbors, have predominantly supported Ukraine. Obviously, they were feeling threatened by neighboring great powers.

We do not need to idealize the UN at all. So far, it really is an ineffective instrument. And even without the problem of the veto power of the permanent members of the Security Council, there are other serious problems with the UN Charter. As Darrel Moellendorf has rightly pointed out, the principle of the sovereign equality of states under the UN Charter means not opposing armed incursions into the territory of other states at the invitation of the official government of that state to suppress revolution, but opposing states' support for revolutionary movements in other states. This contradicts the ideas of socialist internationalism. And in this respect, those leftists who justified the Russian invasion of Syria by referring to the legitimacy of this invasion have actually betrayed socialist principles.

лAs I wrote in another article, perhaps it is now because Russia is invading Ukraine that for the first time in all the years of the UN's existence there is a real chance for reform. In past decades, this was almost impossible, and in a few years, the confrontation between China and the United States may become so acute that it will be impossible again. Therefore, we need to act on this now. And the greatest responsibility lies with the Left that resides in the countries that are permanent members of the Security Council.

26.05.2022
first published in English on *New Politics*

Between Survival and Resistance

Resistance and Solidarity The Left Volunteer Movement in the Russo-Ukrainian War

Vladyslav Starodubtsev

Translated by **Yuliia Kulish**

Before the full-scale war, the Ukrainian left movement was neither considered influential nor had a party or national representation, backboned by a strong community. However, the Russian invasion made leftists look for new contacts and approaches. Spokespeople of leftist and anarchist organizations elaborate on the experience of resistance during the round table *Resistance and Solidarity: Ukrainian Leftists in the War with Russia*.

How did the left adapt to the situation after the full-scale invasion of Russia?

The war shaped a completely different context for our activity. Often, the first challenge was to survive individually. Then comes survival at the organizational level: we needed restructuring to adapt to the wartime that defined new areas of activity.

Anastasia Chebotariova talks about such changes among left-wing feminists.

She is a member of the *Feminist Lodge*, a grassroots activist initiative engaged in the cultural and educational sphere. Also, their community provides humanitarian aid, primarily to female persons.

After February 24, helping with the basic needs in treatment, hygiene and nutrition became a priority for *Feminist Lodge*. The organization reformatted its youth cultural direction to organize humanitarian convoys, particularly to the temporarily occupied territories of the Kherson and Zaporizhzhia Oblasts. In such a way, it expanded the network of contacts with grassroots activists throughout Ukraine. Previously, *Feminist Lodge* worked with an audience already interested in feminism; how-

ever, with the beginning of a full-scale war, the organization encountered new voices among the recipients of humanitarian aid.

Anastasia recalls the reaction of a volunteer who delivered supplies to occupied Berdiansk [a city in Donbas — tr. note], "I thought feminists were into some nonsense, but now I see it's far from the truth."

She emphasizes the importance to stress feminist approaches to aid as they differ from the usual activities of large international funds preferring a hierarchic system, "It is important that our help goes along with our feminist values and principles. Thus, people will have a more positive association with the word "feminism.""

Maksym Shumakov talks about cooperation and opposition to neoliberal reforms.

Maksym is an activist of the socialist public organization *Social Movement*, a left-wing association aimed at creating a political party to represent the left in the Ukrainian political arena.

At the end of February, the very first goal of the organization was to overcome disorientation as the activists ended up in different regions and, therefore, circumstances. Their cooperation, communication, and mutual assistance came to the fore. It was important not only to maintain work efficiency but also to ensure the safety of the members.

Then, *Social Movement* focused on several areas: providing humanitarian aid, promoting a campaign to write off Ukraine's foreign debt, supporting the Ukrainian resistance on the international scene, and fighting against neoliberal reforms. As for the last direction, the organiza-

Vladyslav Starodubtsev is a Ukrainian democratic socialist, social and political activist and historian of Central Eastern Europe.

tion actively provides legal assistance to workers in their struggle for labor rights.

The implementation of neoliberal policies and the state's impotence in fulfilling its social role formed a vacuum filled by decentralized cooperation. According to Maksym, almost all collective groups (people at the front, IDPs, students, workers) have already mastered the cooperation basics. Therefore, it is crucial to develop existing initiatives and connect them so as to gain solidarity. Hence, *Social Movement* holds lectures for IDPs, students, workers, and activists.

This May, *Social Movement* organized two conferences in Lviv. It was an important step to unify Ukrainian left-wing initiatives: in the political and media space and in the field of humanitarian aid. First, the conferences proved the subjectivity of the Ukrainian left and trade unions. Second, they helped to establish cooperation and communication in campaigns, humanitarian convoys, and media work.

Maksym stresses that with the war, usual forms of protest became ineffective. Thus, flash mobs, media work, and legal aid played a leading role in reacting to neoliberal reforms. For example, *Social Movement* held a flash mob called *Don't Hit Me in the Back* that drew attention to the threats posed by the new labor rights laws. Protests and media campaigns in new formats still allow to push the authorities and unite people.

Anastasia Brezina elaborates on the relations between man, nature, and war. Also, she talks about the activities of eco-anarchists.

Anastasia is an activist of *Ecoplatform*, a vegan-anarchist eco-organization that promotes principles of horizontality and evasion from the anthropocentric ideology.

The main goal of *Ecoplatform* is to overcome anthropocentrism. As Anastasia states, this war, through crimes and destruction, showed the atrocities of humans toward nature.

Members of *Ecoplatform* faced the first war day in the queue to join Lviv Teroborona. According to Anastasia, female persons had trouble with this: at first, they were just ignored. That is why male members went to the front, and female activists started volunteering.

At the same time, *Ecoplatform* assisted *Solidarity Collectives* [an anti-authoritarian volunteer network — ed.] in logistics, storage, and sorting of humanitarian aid. Anastasia says they faced a surge of solidarity with locals: even a small team could quickly manage to send aid to hot spots.

Various anarchist and vegan initiatives helped in building a strong communication network. Also, anarchists and vegans that join the Armed Forces of Ukraine foster greater visibility and destigmatization in society.

Activists of the *Ecoplatform* feel inspired by the idea of a grassroots mode of society; however, currently, they observe a common tendency to idealize the state and power structures.

Serhiy Movchan, a member of the anti-authoritarian volunteer network *Solidarity Collectives*, talks about its military and humanitarian activities.

The initiative originated in the network of anarchists, anti-fascists, and anti-authoritarian leftists a few weeks before the start of the full-scale war and was inseparable from the military association. Part of the members decided to create a unit in the Armed Forces of Ukraine, and another one — to engage in humanitarian activities that would provide for the anti-authoritarian leftists at the front.

Solidarity Collectives[1] began to assemble a new network and infrastructure. Over time, the directions expanded to providing humanitarian aid to civilians and engaging in media work. Activists began reaching out to trade unions, which usually did not get help from big funds.

Leftist organizations are trying to keep their identity amidst the diversity of new volunteer initiatives so that the sense of national unity won't replace the organizations' political principles. All participants of the round table highlighted that the war creates a new space for the left, prospects for destigmatization, and strengthening the positions of LGBTQ+ activists, feminists, anarchists, and vegan activists. Helping people and fighting side by side in the army allows for strengthening the left authority and building new contacts. Activists hope this will become a good basis for post-war work and for defending social and economic rights in the future.

Ukrainian leftists vs abstract pacifism of the West. What is the left movement fighting against?

Many Ukrainian leftists orient towards the Western media, as Ukrainian ones are much more challenging due to the activities of the far right, as well as the fact that leftists tend to be associated with pro-Russian forces. According to the speakers, the reaction of the Western left and feminist communities creates obstacles for the Ukrainian left.

Some Western leftists and feminist activists have forgotten one of the most important rules: nothing about us without us. They publish numerous manifestos inviting no representatives of Ukrainian society. We hear calls to lay down arms, return to the Minsk agreements, and slander the Ukrainian leftists for "nationalism"... These things are often shaped like colonial and authoritarian relations: one side explains what the other should do, giving no try to understand it.

As Anastasia Chebotariova points out, this is an issue of power distribution. The Ukrainian left movement found itself in a position where it is necessary to explain the situation over again, but often it seems like serving the international community. We can overcome it by recognizing common values and visions, not competition or opponents. For example, Kurdish feminists understand that not everyone has the privilege of non-violent resistance, but everyone must build relationships based on the equality principle.

Anastasia explains why she does not cooperate with the Russian anti-war feminist resistance that expresses solidarity with Ukrainians. Although they do not influence the war much, their activities have attracted significant attention in the West. The thing is that it is happening at the expense of Ukrainian initiatives becoming less visible. It is more difficult for the West to understand the resistance of the colonized, so they often prefer to give voice to people from empires. Supporting such initiatives only legitimizes spatial inequality and makes Ukrainian feminism less visible.

We are interested in the decolonization of empires (and relations). Now, Ukrainians are fighting against an empire. Leftists and anarchists support movements in Central Asia and other colonized regions because decolonization is the future we can fight for together, not only in the context of the Russo-Ukrainian war.

Answering questions about left-wing pacifism and the call to "put down weapons," Serhiy Movchan emphasized that "practice is the criterion of truth." Some statements of the "anti-war movement" seem good in theory but are far from practice. One cannot put an equal sign (as some leftists in the West like to do) between two "bourgeois" countries where the working class is not in power. After all, there is a big contrast between Ukraine and Russia regarding the democracy level and opportunities for independent organizations.

Today, the very existence of the Ukrainians is under threat. The freedoms of Ukrainian activists would be impossible under the Russian occupation. For us, this war is defensive. One needs to fight against the invader, not against its opposers.

Footnotes

[1] at that time the initiative was called "Operation Solidarity".

09.11.2022

We Must Fight for the Future of Ukrainian Education. Interview with the Priama Diia (the Direct Action) student union

Interviewed by *Commons*

On the eve of September 1st, the Day of Knowledge, *Commons* spoke to activists of the student union *Priama Diia* about the right to education in a country at war. They explain why they decided to relaunch the union, what obstacles there are to protecting students' rights, and share their plans and dreams for the future of Ukrainian education after the war.

The Commons editorial board: *The union's history goes back almost 30 years. Many of our editors and contributors were Priama Diia members during their studenthood. However, in the mid-2010s, the union declined. How did you come up with the idea of reviving it?*

The Priama Diia: The rebirth of the union began with a wave of dissatisfaction with the forthcoming reform. In 2021, the Ukrainian Ministry of Education and Science launched a new reform to optimise higher education establishments: universities that were "unprofitable for the state" would be integrated into more efficient universities. This meant losing the material base of these educational establishments, mass redundancies of teaching staff and the abolition of state scholarships for students. Of the 150 largest state universities, 80 were to remain.

The reform outraged students and teachers, which led to demonstrations in various Ukrainian cities. The most significant action occurred on 2 December 2021, when students and everyone concerned opposed the merger of the Kharkiv National University of Construction and Architecture with the Beketov National University of Oil and Gas. Soon-to-be *Priama Diia* activists also helped to prepare the demonstration. The lack of a powerful trade union and organisational experience was a major obstacle at the time, as the students needed to consider the universality of their problem, had no experience of fighting for their rights regularly and had a vague vision of their objectives. Organisations affiliated with the administration did not want to participate in protest activities, and independent student associations remained silent or supported the neoliberal mantras about the need to privatise education and the whole social sphere in Ukraine.

Legal, economic and educational problems were piling up exponentially. Only the left had a critical vision and an understanding of a valid alternative, but there was no left-wing youth organisation in Ukraine then. We knew the *Priama Diia* union had existed, and we spoke to its former members, who are still influential activists. Their successes and efforts inspired us to recreate the movement. A few months after the autumn demonstrations, the full-scale invasion began. The number of challenges for us increased dramatically. Since then, we have been actively involved in volunteering, helping students at a local level and joining in student actions close to home.

The education system, eroded by years of state irresponsibility, began to writhe in pain. Maintaining a necessary level of learning became almost impossible, as students were in danger every day and, in some parts of Ukraine, directly threatened with death. Evacuation, destruction of housing, eviction from dormitories, loss of contact with parents, loss of jobs and a general lack of stability... In these challenging circumstances, the students also came up against total incomprehension by the university administrations. The level of abuse increased significantly. Many of us felt these problems acutely.

Finally, we analysed the new conditions, pulled ourselves together and realised there was no point in waiting any longer. In February 2023, we, a group of 3 to 5

left-wing activists, launched an open call to students wishing to join the *Priama Diia*. The result was unexpected, as our organisation started growing fast: the lack of access to offline education and the small number of genuinely left-wing organisations in Ukraine played their part — young people were hungry for activism.

C: The Priama Diia in previous generations was an anarcho-syndicalist union. What are your political positions today? How does the current generation of students view left-wing politics?

PD: We are noticing the following trend: since the start of the large-scale invasion, many people, including youth and students, have felt the need to get involved in the social, public and political life of the country. This can be explained in various ways, for example, by the fact that everyone is trying to find their place in the resistance to Russian imperialism, whether through volunteering, organising various training courses or joining the Armed resistance.

Of course, for many, forming a new Ukrainian identity is negative: "We are not-Russia". Whether this is a productive strategy for building a community is another matter. However, it is clear that young people primarily form their worldview by contrasting Russian authoritarianism with democracy, persecution of the gay community with inclusion, and so on. As a result, we are seeing a rise in culturally leftist views among students: these people generally describe themselves as liberals, in the American sense.

That is why we are working mainly with this segment of the public. There is no doubt that *Priama Diia* today continues to demonstrate the need to combine political

and trade union visions in order to organise a powerful student movement. The issues we raise would be superficial if we did not emphasise that our strategic demands are, first and foremost, political. For example, affordable or even free education is a demand for this specific sector, education, but only through an in-depth transformation of the social and political system will such demands take on their whole meaning.

From this point of view, the union comprises two poles which, in our opinion, are not viable without each other: the vast student community, which is directly linked to the experience of the educational process, its shortcomings and deficiencies, and the militant core, which brings a radical political programme and universalises specific problems. This means that to join *Priama Diia*, one does not need to be reading volumes of Proudhon or Marx; one just needs to agree with the minimum requirements, i.e. the inadmissibility of discrimination on several grounds — gender identity, race, etc. — and to be wishing to take action. The militant backbone now includes anarchists, Marxists, social democrats and supporters of more exotic currents of political thought. In short, the Priama Diia is today a left-wing student union in the broadest sense.

C: What political organisations and trends do you follow, both historically and today? Who are your allies in Ukraine and abroad?

PD: On the one hand, we try to experiment with the structure to invent new forms and principles of organisation. This form of political creativity requires a great deal of internal flexibility. For example, to involve the less active participants and coordinate our work, we created the Coordination Headquarters, whose members are elected by sortition (according to the traditions of Antiquity). When we encountered problems in the operation of this body, we would meet to analyse the reasons for them, think about how to overcome the shortcomings, and so on. Today, to a large extent, the Coordination Headquarters works the way we wanted and shows that such "bizarre" and ultra-democratic forms can work — you just have to experiment with and improve them along the way.

On the other hand, when we do not need to reinvent the wheel, we turn to historical experience. The student movement has a long history in different chronological and geographical contexts. By studying this heritage and being aware of the differences with the current situation, we can avoid repeating the same mistakes.

This is how we began to study the student union movement in Quebec, a region where it is still strong today. Since 1968, the province has had a distinctive student association structure that ensures the re-enactment of teaching strikes and general assemblies of teachers and students. We drew inspiration from ASSÉ (the Association pour la solidarité syndicale étudiante), which existed from 2001 to 2019 and had 34 member associations with 56,000 students while remaining left-wing. We continue to study their strategies, tactics and internal organisation, looking for things that can be adapted and work in our context. For example, the concept of 'students as workers' allows us to address several issues in higher education in a different way, creating a space for solidarity not only with other student groups and movements but also with other trade union initiatives: nursing, construction, and those launched by service workers (where students often work part-time because of low stipends).

It is worth noting that we have friendly contacts with the Polish organisation "Koło Młodych", part of the trade union "Inicjatywa Pracownicza", where our activists recently attended a conference, shared their experience and helped organise training. We also have close links with the French student organisation "Solidaires-étudiantes".

In Ukraine, the situation is somewhat different. Most Ukrainian student initiatives, such as the Ukrainian Students for Freedom or the Ukrainian Students League, have fundamentally different principles to ours. The USF is a right-wing libertarian organisation focusing mainly on political issues, leaving social issues aside. Sometimes, their ideological underpinnings produce, in our view, openly anti-student positions: during the reorganisation of the Kharkiv NUBA, in the course of which some members of staff had to lose their jobs and students had to lose their state-funded places, USF refused to cooperate during the protest because it considered this "optimisation" expedient.

Nevertheless, we are happy to cooperate with student councils, organisations and other forms of autonomy that operate within universities. Their actions are admittedly limited, as the university administration governs them, but joint projects and communication are an important part of our work. We need activists through student associations at various universities to find out about problems, corruption and so on. Sometimes, these student associations are not happy to cooperate with us because they find us suspicious, but in general, we often manage to establish communication.

C: Your generation of activists has the most difficult tasks. What issues does Priama Diia deal with? What are your main activities today?

PD: One can divide our tasks into two categories: those related to the state's education policy during the war and those of a more general nature, such as promoting emancipatory tendencies in the organisation of education, the fight against discrimination, eco-activism, and the popularisation of left-wing ideas among young people.

We all know that during martial law, men of military age are not allowed to leave the country. This ban applies to students, whether they are studying abroad or in Ukraine. This state policy considerably hampers the educational process, as students enrolled in foreign educational establishments need to travel to their place of study. In an environment where local universities are systematically underfunded and the level of teaching declines due to overwork, students lose motivation and do not receive all the knowledge they need. As a result, shortly, we will face a shortage of the professionals needed to support Ukraine's society and economy and, hopefully, a successful post-war reconstruction. This is why allowing male students to study abroad is one of the main demands of our union.

In May 2023, we launched the StudAk campaign to fight for the right to take a gap year and enjoy social guarantees provided by the pre-war legislation. University administrations promised students that, after a legal break, they could return to free education, which they had been waiting for. However, in the autumn of 2022, the Department of Education and Science issued Resolution No. 1224, which effectively abolished all state scholarships for these students.

As the first step, we contacted the victims to assess the scale of the problem. To this end, we have sent hundreds of letters to the student councils and rectors of the country's various universities. However, we have not received a significant response (around five replies). We have also contacted foundations to ask them to cover the costs of particularly hard-hit students. In any case, we have not found any support from universities or government agencies. We are now at a crossroads: some see direct action as the last chance to make our voices heard, while others consider contacting the media.

A few days ago, we launched a petition to transform the former Russian embassy building in Kyiv into a community centre. Instead of staying empty or being turned into another shopping centre, this space will become a meeting point where students can share their knowledge and experiences. This will make it easier to generate new ideas and work together to implement them. In addition, the community centre will support people who need help and shelter. If the petition does not receive a large-scale response, we plan to run several rallies to draw attention to the project.

C: Like many other institutions in Ukrainian society, education requires reform. How do you see a positive future for Ukrainian education? In short, how should a university be organised so that young people want to study there?

PD: Our union has strategic, ambitious and even utopian visions. There are several different positions, and we have yet to formulate a single one, although we hope to draft a manifesto setting out the main principles by the end of the year.

Of course, we agree that education should be affordable, even free. On this basis, the members of the *Priama Diia* are building different models. Let me give an example. Universities and the higher education system, in general, play an essential role in the reproduction of society: the knowledge at different levels of practical application that students acquire is used in business, industry, management, politics, etc. The material and political benefits we enjoy as a society are deeply rooted in the education system. Consequently, by studying, writing theses and essays and producing ideas, students do part of the work necessary not only for the development of society but also for its reproduction as such. From this point of view, a student acts like a worker, which means they should not only be able to afford their studies — but also get paid for it. The idea of a student wage is not new. At the height of the student movement in the 1970s, it had many supporters and was a concrete demand for the authorities.

To this strategic vision must be added the fundamental autonomy and democratisation of universities. We do not believe that students are "consumers of education", participants of a market in which knowledge has a utilitarian function. Universities are not supermarkets selling knowledge like biscuits. The knowledge we receive within the higher education system is flexible and is con- stantly being transformed during the learning process. This is how education improves and adapts to demands.

Therefore, students are full participants in this process and should play an appropriate role in managing it. This is not our whims but a matter of improving higher education, which is increasingly urgent in the context of post-war reconstruction.

We need to show the students (including those who left Ukraine) that positive changes are underway in the higher education system. Such transformations are not the fruit of the goodwill of a minister or a president but require a struggle and the involvement of students. Unfortunately, young people today do not see educational problems as exceptional but rather as a regular, "natural" state of affairs. We often hear statements like, "It cannot get any better!" At such times, Mark Fisher's verdict that we have forgotten how to imagine rings true. In order to move things forward, we propose different strategic visions of the ideal education.

Apart from the utopian demands, we acknowledge the challenges that must be dealt with here and now. These trivial problems are the starting point for more critical work: courses lacking syllabi, poorly designed academic calendars, cockroaches in dormitories, and many others. Every little victory revives the organisation and takes it to a new level. For this work "on the ground", we are now decentralising the organisation and registering branches (union sections) at different universities. It is important not only to focus on the problems of Ukrainian education in general but also to work on a small scale.

C: *What do you wish students on 1st September?*

PD: Always to have the power to choose. Choose what you study, who you listen or talk to, and what path you follow. Sometimes, the circumstances leave you little choice and there are thousands of obstacles in your way. That is why we exist as a union, where every student can overcome obstacles and fight for decent education. That is why it is crucial not to succumb to standardisation and "averaging". Let education give you the means to think critically about the social relations surrounding you, overcome inequality, injustice and arbitrariness, and not drag you into a system built on domination and submission.

01.09.2023

Experiences That Should Have Never Happened Again: How Ukrainians Survive the War

Alona Liasheva

Translated by **Olenka Gu**

Russia's invasion has made murder, rape and torture a part of our everyday life. It never ceases to terrify, anger and remind us that we cannot stop fighting. Indeed, those defending us from the invader, those who have lost their loved ones or survived rape and torture, struggle the most. The existence of this suffering, however, does not make all other war experiences less important. Next to the most brutal episodes of the war, we are living our everyday lives, which will not break the internet or become stories for a large Western media, nor will they make one's body tremble with horror. However, no one should ever experience this, nowhere. This text speaks of such 'ordinary' experiences — the experiences that should not have happened.

I am a sociologist. On the first day of the invasion, I sent three letters to the editors of academic journals for which I was writing articles about housing and urban policy in Ukraine. Those letters informed the editors that I was suspending my work on the papers I had been writing for the past year and that, unfortunately, I did not know when I would be back to work. The invasion has changed not just my everyday life but my academic interests as well. Now, I am researching the Ukrainian resistance. Throughout the year, my colleagues and I have conducted in-depth interviews with Ukrainians about what they have been experiencing and how their notions of the world, politics, themselves and others have been changing. Perhaps someday, someone will be able to analyse these experiences and thoughts, identify trends, and even look at what happened from different angles. But for now, every story only adds to the unambiguity of my already black-and-white world, the world in which there is good, and there is evil it must defeat.

Therefore, in this text, there will be no analysis — instead, there will be a direct speech of Ukrainians who have witnessed occupation and hostilities. The interview quotes are unedited so that readers can see not only what people say about their experiences but also how[1] they say it. Vivid emotional reactions, such as laughter or sad sighs, are also indicated in the quotes. The interview transcripts were anonymised to ensure participants' safety, so you will see that names of people or locations are hidden behind asterisks or replaced by a description in square brackets.

All the heroes of this text are very different: they do different jobs and speak different languages; they have faced the full-scale invasion in the territories controlled by Ukraine as well as in the territories controlled by Russia; they have voted for different presidential candidates, explain the invasion differently, and their opinions about the Ukrainian authorities differ, too. What unites them is that they are reinventing their lives, ruined by the war, under new conditions.

Some of the research participants have survived occupation. Considering the hazard people faced under occupation, we did not invite them to an interview until after deoccupation or evacuation took place. Another reason for abandoning fieldwork in the occupied territories was that, in the case of online interviewing, it is harder to support a person when they feel emotionally distressed. No sociological data is worth retraumatising research participants or putting them in danger.

The following stories will appeal to different readers in different ways. If you are reading this text in Ukrainian, you or your loved ones have most likely experienced something similar. Let these stories remind us that our pain as well as our resistance are collective. If you are

Alona Liasheva is a member of the editorial team of the *Commons*, sociologist, researcher of urban political economy. Now she's doing research on war everyday life and Ukrainian resistance.

reading this text in English, this is your opportunity to find out what the everyday reality of war looks like and what Russia has brought us in addition to death and destruction. These stories provide answers to questions about why Ukrainian society does not want to capitulate, why many people do not leave the country (even if they have the opportunity), and why Ukrainians often are not ready to look at current events from different perspectives.

Living in frontline cities and villages

Since 24 February 2022, many cities and villages have become frontline. Even though those places are not occupied, people there live in tremendous danger due to intense shelling, lose access to basic goods and services (such as water, food, medicine and lighting in the streets and at home), live in complete uncertainty regarding tomorrow day... The list is endless. Frontline areas, including such large cities as Kharkiv and Kherson, are attacked the most, and the enemy's artillery can often reach them. The latter increases the risks tenfold.

The hostilities have completely changed the course of everyday life. A woman who had fled a frontline village in Mykolaiv Oblast told us that on the first day of the invasion, she did not expect the war to come to her village as there were no military or industrial facilities there. What concerned her most was that her daughter lived in a big city. But the very next day, the situation changed:

'Everything was quiet and peaceful, we didn't hear those rocket launches, but on the twenty... fifth, I guess, of February, we saw the rockets on our territory with our own eyes, they were flying very low. And we realised that the war... had come to our house. In the beginning... the first three or four days, I think, everyone in my village thought that it would pass us over, that we wouldn't... that the Russian troops wouldn't come to us, but just in three days, they came... Life drastically changed: we found ourselves without lighting, without [mobile] connection... For the first three and a half weeks, we lived there knowing that they were near us but they weren't entering our village. It was winter, we didn't have heating even though we had gas. But almost everyone had double-circuit [electric] boilers which didn't work. There was no electricity, no lighting, and we could only read news on our phones sometimes when there was an opportunity... We would sleep altogether, getting together in one house 'cause we were less scared that way.'

In the next weeks, the shelling only intensified:

'Well, of course, I was scared. It was scary seeing those huge pillars of rockets fly above you, right at the level of your house, and you fall behind a large settee, throwing it, we (smiles) would move it away in a second to hide behind it and wait it out because those were flying. Now, I see the rockets fly kind of higher, but then, they would fly right into buildings. Those pillars.'

Later in the interview, she said that shelling like that had killed some of the women she knew, civilians. Those events made her flee to the west of the country. After Kherson was liberated, this woman and many other residents of her village started coming back, rebuilding their homes, settling matters and restoring trade.

Another research participant is a school teacher who has fled to the west of the country from a big frontline city. At the beginning of the invasion, she decided to stay as relocation seemed a way too complicated process to her. She also wanted to be closer to her husband, who had decided to join the armed forces. Several weeks later, a rocket hit the yard of her tower block but, fortunately, did not explode. The woman, her daughter and her grandson were unharmed. That night they made a decision to leave. Although right now the family is in relative safety, they continue to watch their hometown being destroyed and people they knew being killed. This is how she described her worst experience:

'Boys are clearing [the rubble], like, emergency servicemen, and they are crying 'cause what they're finding… And what was the worst — we found a notebook from our school… in a different neighbourhood. And the notebook was covered in blood. We realised that had happened to a student, we didn't figure out who that was. Maybe the notebook had been there for a long time, maybe someone used to be a student, uh-huh. Well, that was a shock.'

Living under occupation

Many Ukrainians found themselves on the other side of the frontline. That meant not only the proximity of hostilities and the lack of basic goods but also the constant violence of the occupiers. A man who stayed in Bucha to look after his parents and domestic animals described to us his life during the occupation. Every day was a separate dreadful day to live through. Some days felt like the last of his life. Poor connection made those feelings worse. Under such conditions, he had to compose a picture of the hostilities from the news his neighbours were retelling as well as from the shelling sounds. All that remained was to believe and wait. Believing and waiting was all that remained.

'Some days were dreadful. I don't know, some days were really grim, there were shootings and everything, yeah, there were such days. And there was this feeling, like, this day may be the last day of my life. Yeah, and there were calmer days, like a bit of peace, and it was kind of good, quiet. But quiet days were dreadful, too. 'Cause after silence, something horrible can happen. [pauses] 'Cause you know that they might be delivering more weapons or something else. Yeah, that's how I felt. So every day was, how do I put it, a separate dreadful day in my life. It's terrifying.'

A daily schedule had to be adjusted to the shellings. Between shellings, one had to manage to prepare food, feed domestic animals (sometimes, also those of the neighbours who had left), turn on a generator to pump water, go find a place where there is mobile connection and try to call relatives or listen to radio news, which was rarely possible. And as soon as the sounds of artillery were heard — run to the basement.

'Over time, we learnt when it "begins." We knew when shelling would begin and when we could have breakfast, lunch and dinner. I mean, they would attack in ac-

cordance with a schedule. The funniest thing was that it would start at five in the morning, they were shooting and shooting, until about eight or nine o'clock… That's it, you can go in the street, you can walk in the street, go feed [animals]. I mean, we would feed animals here and there, the ones left. … At lunchtime — exactly at lunchtime — we would turn a generator on and pump some water. And, while you're pumping the water, for those ten to twenty minutes, you're trembling. 'Cause they were walking around, and if they heard the noise of a generator, that meant what? Petrol. And if there's petrol… And we had just one tank of petrol, twenty litres. We treasured it like the apple of our eye because no one knew how long we were meant to be like that.'

Everyday issues were not the worst thing during the occupation — it was the life under the occupation regime itself and communication with the occupiers. People were forced to constantly hide at home, going outside as seldom as possible, risking their lives. The occupiers would constantly question, search, humiliate and abuse them. The man I spoke to in Bucha told me that those things were often done 'for fun':

'Those tower blocks, there were eighteen floors… they were on the roof. We could see them, they were often on that roof. So, they started shooting at us, you know, just for fun. Like, above our heads, not at us, but just to scare us. We hear this sound and see the smoke. And suddenly — the whistle, and it blows next to us.'

This is how he described questioning:

'So, they were asking questions, very tricky questions. He [a relative] got it immediately. They ask, "Who is Bandera?" He thinks, "Well, if I say that he's a national hero, I'll be screwed up, they'll just shoot me." So he goes, "Back when I studied at school, that was a nationalist, and now I've got no idea, I'm not interested in that, I do my things." — "How did Ukraine emerge?" He thinks, "If I say it's an independent state, it'll be…" He started answering, in Russian, "There was the Soviet Union. Then, there was the Russian Federative Socialist Republic and Ukrainian Socialist Republic, as well as Georgian and Belarusian, and then the Soviet Union Collapsed, and now we've got Ukraine, Georgia, Belarus, Russia. Separated." And it worked, they didn't touch him. Then there were other questions. And he said he'd realised that they were asking loads of provocative questions which, if you answer them straightforward, like, if you say that Ukraine is an independent country, — you're dead.'

On mobilisation, hiding in the occupied territories and escaping from there

Ukrainians living in DPR and LPR mark the beginning of the full-scale invasion as 18th February instead of

24th. Many did not believe that the war could develop into a full-scale one; thus, they did not evacuate when there still was the opportunity. A young man who had been hiding from mobilisation in DPR for five months until he managed to escape explains the circumstances that made him realise the invasion would take place eventually:

'It's the 19th of February, my best friend and I are at work, and we get a call from our deputy director: "Boys, tonight you have to come to the military commissariat with your belongings." I tell her, "What am I supposed to say to this?" She goes, "Well, I can't tell you anything, but you heard me, you got the information." I tell her, "Well, I heard you, that's all I can say." We realise something shitty is coming, and it's the 20th, Saturday. I say, "B***, let's go now, screw it, I don't care if we're fired or not, I don't give a shit, let's go home right now, pack our stuff and look for a way to leave." That was *mogilisation*[2], when they started recruiting those *mobics*. So, that's what we did. I pulled him, we took off and ran home. That's it — in half an hour, people with guns came to the [institution] where we worked and took all the men away. That half an hour saved us. We come home and start searching — through all the channels, through our acquaintances — how we can leave. We start getting messages, like, we know a woman who works at a military commissariat, she's a boss of some sort: "Guys, it'll be alright, they'll just take some pictures of you and let you go." I was already alert and understood how the stupid system works, so I said, "No, we're not going anywhere."'

His partner, who also stayed and looked after him for the five months as she was able to go outside once in a while, describes what it was like for her and how the mobilisation of men was happening:

'I stayed at home with the guys because there was shelling and I was scared, and eventually I came under fire. … We were really worried that they could take the boys away. And if I met someone I knew, I would normally go to a shop wearing a mask and a hood because I'd told everyone that I left with the boys, like, we'd crossed the border… Of course, the local shopkeepers knew everything: "How are the boys, they weren't taken?" Something like that. Everything I saw and heard was conversations in shops, like, two women are standing and a saleswoman comes up to them, and the woman who came to the shop to buy stuff is telling them about another guy who was taken, and how he was given a summons right in the shop. In the beginning, they would just hand in the summons, and later, they started packing people. They would take people from buses and then, they would go from flat to flat. Later, provocations started, like, they said there would be evacuation of the building, like, something happened, something's burning or there's been an acci-dent, so that all the guys come outside, and they would catch them at the entrance. And we were freaking out, too, we would barricade our front door with a safe and close the peephole, we didn't turn the lights on. That was so much pressure… That was really tough, yeah.'

Five months later, the checkpoints became less strict, so they managed to cross the border and flee through Russia:

'Yeah, the worst checkpoint was when I was lying under the seat, I was hiding, packed like, I don't know, like, I'm not a religious person but then, I almost read a prayer. I was scared as fuck. And finally, the worst thing — that checkpoint, and those from DPR… what are they called… *commendachi*, yeah. Those who stop all the cars at the border and catch everyone… So, this dude who was driving us, he stopped as close to the barrier as possible. He turned with his back, that was funny, too. Like (*laughs*), I'm lying, like this, hiding, he's turning, and I can feel with my body that he's turning or something… And he goes, "When I say run — you run." Like, you get out, grab the suitcases — we had two suitcases — get out, grab the suitcases and run. I get up and he says, "Let's go, now, run." I get out fast, grab the suitcases and run… I run towards them and he shouts, "The other way, you dumbass!" (*laughs*) I turn around and run in the opposite direction. It's like getting into America from Mexico, I think, it's much harder from Mexico. Well, in Mexico, you realise you can get in jail. And here, I mean, one way or another — you'll die and… For fucking what? I mean, I'm completely against this. I don't want to be taken by the DPR. The Territorial Defence [in Ukraine] — okay, in that case, I wouldn't be resisting. But when you're taken by the fucking DPR and sent to die as fucking cannon fodder — that's completely fucked up.'

On mutual aid and resistance

Many Ukrainians, who before the full-scale invasion had never engaged in activism, began to help both civilians and the army. This is the direct speech of a girl who, with the beginning of the invasion, felt that she could not stay out of politics and reorganised her business into a volunteer project:

'In the beginning of the war, I was out of town for a week 'cause I went to visit my mum, and then it wasn't possible to get back. I wanted to go back to [city] on the very first day, no matter what, but the bridge was blown up, and I managed to get home only on the 8th of March. I went to the kitchen right away and started cooking. I was feeding elderly people nearby and processing some requests from Telegram, also from some grandmothers and grandfathers, buying crops and bread in 'Silpo'[3] to give them humanitarian aid. I had some money left, like, a couple of thousands [UAH], and I spent it from our fund. And I started posting on Instagram, like, you can donate, and you can text me and I'll be cooking for you and your relatives, and we'll be delivering it around [the city]. I found a guy, my former client, who had volunteers with cars, and they were delivering lunches around the whole city until curfew.'

The man from Bucha also shared his experience of solidarity with other people living under occupation. His family had gots that gave milk. They started sharing it with others. Through such a network, he managed to obtain insulin for his mother:

'The goats gave birth, they started milking. And my parents were milking them. So, we had milk, and we would share it with people. We would also share other food and whatever we had that we didn't need. Later, of course… My mum was almost running out of insulin because, well, she has this problem, and… Sister-in-law said that, yeah, back when there was the occupation, that humanitarian help was delivered or something, that it was being delivered somehow and distributed at the hospital. But it was really hard to get there. And once, that man, the one with wood, was passing by. We gave him milk and asked if he knew anything about humanitarian aid being delivered, and medicines. He said, "Yes, I heard about that, which meds do you need?" He asked my mum to give him a list of the meds she needed. She wrote the list, gave it to him. And the next day, they brought insulin and other meds and everything. I mean, well, not all the meds, but most importantly, there was insulin, thank God. We calmed down. 'Cause mum, she was just about… Plus, we had no syringes and only one needle, which was so dull it could barely pierce. That was really harsh — we still had insulin but almost no syringes left. Thank God that man brought the insulin, and it got a bit better. People here were trying to help each other whenever they saw someone in need, to pass each other things, whatever they could. Of course, walking in the street, it was more or less not scary only during the quiet hours.'

During this year, solidarity networks were established both within the civilian population and between civilians and the military. People who found themselves under occupation were trying to pass on information to the Armed Forces of Ukraine. This is obviously very dangerous. Here is what the research participant from Bucha told us about such an experience:

'We swapped Viber for Signal because Signal, people said, has better protection, and it's harder to hack it. There, we didn't add any other people, and we would chat there. Tanks, let's say, tanks or cars are riding there, shootings or something. And then, there were people who would pass on the information to the Territorial defence or to the military. We were trying to help and inform in that way. … And the military equipment we took pictures of and exchanged with each other — we had to delete those 'cause if they saw that kind of information on your mobile phone, they could, as the saying goes, execution on the spot.'

Every so often, participants would tell us that they hide from their relatives what they really do not to worry them. A volunteer who came to the east of Ukraine from the west to evacuate civilians from the war zone confessed: 'When I come here to volunteer, I don't… Well, I come up with different stories about how I help rebuild houses in central Ukraine or something.'

Almost every participant has a relative or friend who joined the Territorial Defence without any previous experience. Supporting military people — those one personally knows or not — becomes a part of one's life:

'People who'd never seen weapons, and when there are just eight guns in your village, and they all want to join the Territorial Defence. And what will they do there against heavy machinery? … When they went at tanks with Molotov cocktails, and three men died at once. Among them was one of the best kids' football coaches, he led them into attack… Well, that was also shocking to me that… I, I didn't think that the Territorial Defence could be of any use to our country. But it turned out that many of them are now fighting and protecting me. V***, a friend of mine, he joined the Territorial Defence in the first days, he defended our village from day three, and now he's at war. Well, I'm proud of him. Because he used to be a truck driver who worked abroad, and he went [to war] 'cause he's got two kids.'

Perhaps, the most incomprehensible thing to an outside observer is that, while supporting and participating in the resistance, Ukrainians remain critical of the government and its decisions. Our research participants were dissatisfied with the way the mobilisation was being carried out, criticised the restrictions on travelling abroad, noted the problems with the provision of the army, spoke about their unwillingness to join the army and the fear that they might be forced to, and complained that the authorities did not ensure evacuation. Expectedly, but symptomatically, the topic of politicians' corruption constantly came up in the interviews, even though the word 'corruption' did not appear in our questions. People also resented the renaming of streets and the demolition of monuments to Russian figures. And it is not only a matter of social conflicts regarding specific policies. In the conversations, a narrative emerged that the president's support is rather conditional and temporary.

Ukrainian internal political processes during the war deserve detailed and, most importantly, long-term research as Ukrainians' political views have drastically changed — and will continue to change. It cannot be otherwise in times of historical upheavals. After the first ten interviews, I was no longer surprised that the father of an 'Azov' soldier defends Pushkin, that a person deliberately switches to Ukrainian language and listens to Russian-speaking Arestovych, and that a Russian-speaking Ukrainian dreams of the 'collapse of Russia'. In regard to our future, not only political contradictions are crucial, but also the readiness and willingness to be involved in discussing them and to defend our interests.

The first interviews were collected in the first two months of the invasion. When our team was working on the interview guide, we had doubts about whether people would be ready to talk about domestic policy and express criticism about Ukrainian authorities. Those doubts have been completely dispelled. Now (just like a year ago), sociologists rarely face unwillingness to openly discuss politics — rather the opposite. Unfortunately, nothing is more politicising than bombs.

This text cannot have conclusions. That is because the experiences collected here have not been fully lived through and reflected on. During this year, something happened that should have never happened again. The wounds will take long to heal and might never heal completely. But they give us a chance that sometimes, the 'never again' does not happen again. What we can do is continue to listen to each other, and the world — to Ukrainian voices.

Footnotes

[1] The participants of our research spoke different languages (Ukrainian, Russian and Surzhyk), and it was important to us to preserve the features of their speech — a representation of different geographies and backgrounds — in the interview transcripts. However, in the English version of the article, the unique features of speech are lost in translation.

[2] Mogilisation — a word used by Russian and Ukrainian speakers to describe the aggressive mobilisation in Russia, DPR and LPR; the term combines the words 'mobilisation' and 'grave' ('mogila' or 'mohyla' in Russian or Ukrainian respectively). — TN

[3] A chain of supermarkets in Ukraine.

01.03.2023

The data for this article was collected and processed by Alona Liasheva, Olenka Gu, Iryna Shostak and Kateryna Turenko. This data was collected, and publication was produced as part of the research project 'Comparing Protest Actions', which is organised by the Research Centre for East European Studies at the University of Bremen with financial support from the Volkswagen Foundation, which is not affiliated to the car manufacturer of the same name.

Six Cats, Thirty People, Four Mortar Shells. Two Weeks in the Occupied Kyiv Suburb

Evheny Osievsky

For almost two weeks — from February 24th to March 10th — me, thirty other people, and six cats were living in the dormitory of Kyiv-Mohyla Academy in the township of Vorzel', an administrative part of neighbouring Irpin', so a suburb of Kyiv's suburb. The majority of the building's denizens moved out throughout the first couple of days of the Russian-Ukrainian war; I was among those who believed the quiet sleepy Vorzel', once famous for its health resorts, would be a safe haven. I was proven wrong, and quite spectacularly so. Soon nearby Bucha and Hostomel' became the arenas of heavy fighting. The only way to Kyiv led through them. Approximately on day four, we realized we were cut off. As the week wore off, we found ourselves under occupation.

Superlatives of war

War, it turns out, comes in shades and degrees. You go to sleep in the evening still reading about military clashes in the news; hear distant explosions the next day; feel the window panes shaking for the first time; realize that the place you have been calling home for the last seven years is surrounded by invaders; see the columns of enemy tanks from the window of your room; and end up under mortar shelling. All of this is war. Its comparatives and superlatives bleed into each other, what may have once seemed like a watershed moment becomes routine. You can sleep under artillery fire, you can read under artillery fire, you can do chores under artillery fire.

Strictly speaking, at first there were twenty-eight, not thirty; twenty-eight students, PhD candidates, refugees from Donbass. On the eighth day of our isolation, in the afternoon, a car emerged abruptly in front of the fence of our premises. Four people rushed out and spent several minutes racing back and forth through the street before we realized they were civilians and needed help. They stayed with us thereafter. The story they told: a family of four, three women and an elderly man, spent a week in the basement of their house before picking what they believed was a quiet day to try to "break through." At a circular turn, some four hundred meters shy of the town limit, they caught sight of the column of Russian soldiers, who fired a flurry of gunshots into the car. Several bullets pierced the windshield, leaving a light scratch on the face of the driver. Miraculously, nobody was killed or injured.

Their cats were called Cindy and Yasya. An adorable white kitten and a belligerent Cornish Rex in her twilight years with steely eyes of a Viking crippled by a stroke, the creature that terrified our only male cat and the present writer.

Animals, it turned out, adapted at lightning speed. In just a few days' time both of my lady-cats learned to crawl under the bed as soon as the strafing started. Later, conversely, they stopped paying attention to explosions, even those happening nearby, and continued eating, sleeping, or grooming though the cannonade. Same with people. If at first almost everyone raced to the ground floor, heading for the self-styled bomb shelter within the first echoes of the rafale, in the space of several days many chose to sleep in their rooms at night even when the sky towards Kyiv blossomed with a mud-orange glow as the aviation was doing its job somewhere in the dark. When the battle sounds ceased, we would go out to count "pryl'oty," the hits. In total, four mortar — or so I was told — shells ended up on our premises. The closest one hit the fencepost, about thirty meters from my room. It cost us half a dozen broken windows. This counts as "lucky" by

Evheny Osievsky was a journalist and anthropologist. He died on May 22, 2023 after a landmine flew into his trench and exploded.

wartime criteria. Several nearby houses received direct hits and turned into smoldering ruins. We do not know whether anyone was inside at the time.

Communities on the bookshelf; communities under shelling

Electricity and running water disappeared on the third day. My ability to read came back on the fourth. We were not allowed to have light — even candlelight — at night-time, so our biological clocks eventually synchronized with the solar one: getting up at dawn, going to sleep soon after dusk. We used firewood to cook, wells to get drinking water.

Throughout the fifteen days between the start of war and evacuation I finished a monograph about the construction of gender in Vanuatu; a popular work dedicated to the history of the "Sacred Band," the insuperable ancient Greek military unit comprised of three hundred lovers; and swallowed several hundred pages of a classical sociological study on the life of neurobiological lab. Yet, it was the *Fragments of an Anarchist Anthropology* by Leftist social theoretician David Graeber that provided the most productive foil for my Vorzel' experience.

Graeber's book is more of a manifesto than a full-fledged conceptual exposition; slightly more than a hundred pages in its Prickly Paradigm Press edition. (Due to the systematic omission of this latter detail, the present author managed to garner the genuine admiration of his isolation comrades: "You read the whole thing in only two days?") Graeber undertakes an anarchist revision of the history of anthropology and reminds us how many of its classics — Radcliffe-Brown, Mauss, Clastres — harbored communitarian worldviews and moral compasses.

He presents the ethnographic archive as a treasure trove of experiences and social experiments in non-hierarchical, even anti-hierarchical arrangements of human commonwealth. Towards its end, *Fragments* turns into an apologia of spontaneous creative impulses of egalitarian communities — Antiglobalists in Seattle, Zapatists in Latin America, the peasants of Madagascar. These forces, the author claims, can offer an alternative to the societies of coercion and discrimination; sprouts of freer, more just, more utopian — Graeber does not shy away from the word — futures are being created in their furnaces as we speak.

As I was reading *Fragments*, our little group gathered foodstuffs left by the residents of the dormitory and organized a community kitchen. Tasks were divided organically, without voting, drawing schedules, or codifying charters — people silently assumed responsibilities for the things they were able to take care of. Some woke up before sunrise to start a fire and heat up the water for tea. Some cooked. Yet others cleaned the bomb shelter. Even the most inept and least adapted individuals found roles to fill — say, being a water carrier. Every weird hobby, every dent on the surface of somebody's biography found their beneficial uses. Archaeologists, people with rich experience of living in the wild, took care of the bonfire. Refugees from Donbass taught us how to lie down correctly during shelling. Plans to have a collective yoga class were repeatedly discussed — after all, we had a professional yoga instructor in our midst — but never came to fruition because of the consensus of laziness. So Graeber is right, then? Under the repressive scurf of late capitalism — the beach of a society of equals? No. Not exactly.

Gradually, it became apparent that not everybody had found their calling. A number of people — doubtlessly a minority, but a statistically significant one — did not choose any role and, it appeared, had no problem whatsoever with it. Moreover, even among the actively engaged, the measure of effort, put into the common cause, varied widely. I would be happy to be mistaken, but in the long run such emergent inequalities would have probably led to conflicts. In addition, the responsibilities inside the community got divided along the lines inherited from antebellum life. Most notably — the lines of gender. Even though both sexes participated equally in the preparation of food, it was girls and women who nearly always washed the dishes. And these were, mind, "progressive" students of one of the country's top universities.

Something similar was taking place within the township itself. On the one hand, Vorzel' community cooperated and self-organized. People brought food and clothes to the local maternity hospital, neighbouring communities-under-shelling shared information and supplies. On the other hand, long before the beginning of mass barrages, the local diaspora of spirits aficionados broke into two alcohol shops. Conversely, the worker (or, perhaps, the manager) of the town's cosmetic store did not simply refuse to open her shop to the people when the connection with the outside world was irrecoverably lost, but even refused to sell items — female hygiene products included — for cash. On balance, as my comrade from *Commons* editorial team Aliona Liasheva observed in the case of war-transmogrified Lviv, Vorzel' under Russian occupation witnessed the simultaneous unfolding of several directly opposite processes. Crisis, it appears, reveals both the best and the worst that people are and can be.

Manifestations of life

There was something sinister and methodical about the way Vorzel' was gradually cut out of the canvas of Kyiv's woods and suburbs, something akin to an autopsy in the anatomic theatre performed on a live animal. As our energy supplies dwindled and telephones refused to work, we became increasingly starved for information, increasingly dependent on hearsay and fragments of the speech of our loved ones. Since day two of the Russian occupation, stories about murdered civilians started to circulate. Stories about the sniper preying on the town from his post on the bridge atop the railway lines. Stories about the command center of the occupants inside Vorzel's town hall. The latter turned out to be untrue. We are still not sure about the rest.

We told each other about the burial mounds of the late Iron Age, the proper way to conduct laboratory analyses for gonorrhea and chlamydia, about drawing natal charts. Cigarettes transformed into a universal currency, while paper money lost all its value and meaning. The warm days of winter passed and were replaced by cold spring with below zero temperatures and surprise morning snowfalls. We were told about the grotesque streets of Bucha, covered with Russian machines of war and human bodies. Big beautiful dogs with sad eyes left by their owners started coming to our kitchen.

Life under occupation goes on. If not exactly uninterrupted, then at least untamed. Throughout the time of isolation, a new couple emerged in our shelter (in defiance of a two-week-long absence of a shower). Fifteen children were born in the maternity hospital down the street. On a penultimate day, when the evacuation of Vorzel' was already under way, I accidentally met a Canadian who did not speak a single word of Ukrainian but was smiling and looked unreasonably happy against the background of the ragtag masses of townspeople who had gathered to wait for the humanitarian corridor. This man — David is my best guess — came to Ukraine at the very end of the last year, despite the warnings of his government and other world leaders about the imminent war. He did not regret his choice. Why? David (or was it Stephen?) showed me an engagement ring on his left hand. "Came to marry her. Proposed two times, both times she agreed. Heard about war, realized I might never see her again if I won't come. She's an opera singer, you know!" Stephen (or maybe David, after all) and his bride-to-be were sheltering in Vorzel's church, together with a large group of locals. I insistently recommended him not to utter a single word out loud in the case he came across Russians: "Pretend you are a deaf-mute, use sign language." Technically, of course, he would have to invent a sign language of his own.

21.03.2022

Destruction of Signs, Signs of Destruction

Volodymyr Artiukh

Russia's president justified his attack on Ukraine by referring to denazification, while Ukrainian inhabitants and authorities compare the behaviour of Russian soldiers with that of German Nazi occupiers. The memory of the Second World War shared by the citizens of both countries could not avoid instrumentalization, especially around the Day of Remembrance and Reconciliation celebrated in Ukraine (May 8) and the Victory Day in Russia and Ukraine (May 9). There is, however, a notable asymmetry in how the Ukrainian and the Russian side use the heritage of the victory over Nazi Germany. Both are selective, but whereas the Ukrainian side fights iconic signs and appeals to visceral bodily experience through indexes, the Russian side relies almost exclusively on symbols devoid of any relation to lived experience. I will sketch the relations between war-related destruction, lived experienced, and ideology in this blog post dedicated to the defeat of Nazi Germany 77 years ago.

The May 8 speech given by Ukraine's president Zelensky is a good illustration of Ukraine's official aesthetics of the ongoing war in relation to the WWII. In this carefully directed video he stands in front of a destroyed residential building in the town of Borodianka, Kyiv region. It was one of the first to be occupied by the Russian army in an attempt of a pincer movement towards Kyiv and remained under occupation for over a month. Most of the buildings have been destroyed in artillery and aerial strikes; although over 80% of the town's 13000 inhabitants managed to escape, several hundred civilians are considered dead. Previously Zelensky said that the scale of destruction in this town was even worse than in the infamous Bucha, and in this video, he calls the blackened rubble 'a witness' that has become 'numb'. This year's presidential address is accompanied by the endless photographic imagery of destruction and stresses the emptiness of ideological commitments: 'Can the golden words become worthless?'

The black and white video consists of a juxtaposition of images and stories of the destruction wrought by the Nazis in WWII and the contemporary destruction by the Russian army. No political symbols are displayed. Zelensky uses the story from Borodianka itself, the settlement that was once destroyed by the German army and has now been destroyed again by Russians. As the drone camera zooms in on the exposed interiors behind the fallen wall, Zelensky describes in detail the remnants of the flats behind him, speculating that the people who lived there put pictures of the WWII veterans on the walls, then he goes on to recall how the German army destroyed over 200 houses in this town, burned people alive and took men for forced labour.

These two temporally distant pictures converge into the recollection of the early morning of February 24 this year when Ukrainians woke up to explosions from Russian missile strikes. This emotional description of waking up before dawn on the first day of war evokes in the post-Soviet memory the WWII song 'On June 22, at four o'clock sharp' that contains the words 'Kiev was bombed, and we were told the war has started.' The reference to suffering, fear, and disbelief at the cruelty of the invaders also brings to memory the Perestroika era movie 'Come and see', devoid of heroism and lofty rhetoric, which focuses on the bodily experience of war by a Belarusian boy. Thus, this is a visceral memory policy that appeals to people's immediate lived experience under destruction by constructing a series of indexical rather than iconic signs accompanied by person-centric commentary.

Volodymyr Artiukh. Social anthropologist researching working class and migration in Eastern Europe

The second component of the speech was an appeal to contemporary participation in the war — people who fight Russians now are compared to the people who fought Nazism in WWII. The destruction of Warsaw is compared to the erasure of Mariupol, the devastation of Coventry is compared to the bombardment of Kharkiv followed by a series of geographical-historical analogies between various Ukrainian locations and those in the UK, France, the Netherlands, Czechoslovakia, Greece, and other European countries. Zelensky reiterated this parallelism in his May 9 Victory Day video, where he presented a narrative of Ukrainian people defending their fatherland within the anti-Hitler coalition and denied Russian authorities the heritage of the victory. Thus, this line of comparison short-circuits the personal and the global bypassing the national political history, as if Soviet Ukraine never existed and the Soviet Union as a whole was never part of the anti-Nazi coalition.

Russian propaganda follows a drastically difference line. Whereas Ukrainian propaganda erases Soviet symbols and appeals to bodies and affects, Russian propaganda stuffs the symbolic space with iconic signs while erasing bodies, both literally and discursively. After Russian tanks rolled into Kherson region waving red flags, the newly occupied territories in the east and south of Ukraine have been planted with Soviet flags and symbols.

The most recent darling of the Russian propaganda is a film still of an old lady with a red flag, now reproduced in countless banners, wall paintings, statues, and even potentially on a space rocket. This image comes from a video apparently made by Ukrainian soldiers, who approach an old village lady and offer her a package with food. She mistakenly thought they were Russian troops, so she greeted them with a red flag. Ukrainian soldiers trample the flag, and the old lady refuses to take the package. This story has a continuation, which is also filmed by the Ukrainian army. Although it has been impossible to verify independently, the story presented by the Ukrainian Centre for Strategic Communication and Info-Security wants us to believe that the house of this old lady had been destroyed by Russian shelling, and the woman with her husband were offered refuge in Kharkiv. On camera, the old lady says that she is not happy with being used as a symbol of the war and that she came out with a red flag only to ensure that Russian soldiers would not shoot at her. The video shows the rubble that remained of her house.

The story of this old lady, regardless of the degree to which the sequel was staged, shows that the Russian propaganda, as it were, follows Roland Barthes' analysis of the myth as if it was a textbook; lived experiences, life stories behind symbols do not matter. The iconic and symbolic signs, fluid, devoid of any coherent ideology behind them and articulated for the demand of the moment, erase life trajectories, function as a brand, a sign of ownership and belonging. For the Ukrainian side, the present experience of suffering and destruction as represented in the indexical signs of photos and videos should speak for itself, historical analogies should spring to existence beyond symbols and icons that are being destroyed as signs of the centuries-old oppression within the campaigns for decommunization and de-Russification. However, there is a notable similarity beyond this asymmetry: between bodies and signs, the indexical and the iconic, there is a very thin symbolic layer of meaning that consists of slogans rather than a coherent ideology. Russians use non-ideological symbols to destroy bodies,

Ukrainians use destroyed non-ideological bodies to fight symbols.

Indeed, many have been puzzled by the Latin letter Z that has become the symbol of the Russian invasion. It has first been noticed in late January on Russian military vehicles near Ukraine's border. Even then it was unclear what it was supposed to mean. After the invasion begun, this letter started appearing on the streets of Russian cities and towns, on cars, children were made to form this letter with their bodies. However, even Russian propagandists are bewildered by the fact that a letter of the Latin alphabet came to the centre of propaganda campaign in support of the war.

According to the Russian sociologist Andrey Pertsev, there is no deep ideological meaning behind this letter, and there is no need for such meaning. Russian authorities do not bother about having a coherent ideology or inculcating it in the population. The population, in turn, does not need to understand or explain anything: the polls and qualitative studies show that Russians' opinion is fragmented in what concerns the causes and the goals of the war. The authorities do not need active support, the population is not willing to resist. Z is an ideal free-floating signifier, but nobody even bothers to assemble a coherent ideology around it, to do the populist political work that Ernesto Laclau and Chantal Mouffe might have expected to happen. It is a symbol so devoid of meaning that it verges on an index. Z points to pure power and a pure demand for obedience. There is no need to put on special glasses to see 'obey' behind seductive phrases. Obedience itself is the ideology. 'Z' appeared as an identifier of the military coercion, and it turned into an index of the political and police coercion.

This is probably one of the defining features of the regimes that started appearing in post-Soviet space since 2014 in reaction to the real or perceived threat of popular protests. I would call such forms of governance 'anti-Maidan' regimes in reference to their first legitimizing narrative as opposing Ukraine's Maidan uprising of 2013/2014. First, these were the LNR/DNR, where disparate identities, sentiments, strivings, and nostalgias were kept together by the perpetual state of emergency and constant repressions. Then, there was the post-2020 Belarus, which switched from authoritarian populism to an outright dictatorial police state. Then Russia itself turned to a police state exposing post-fascist tendencies and installed a repressive occupation regime in the newly conquered territories in Ukraine. What unites these regimes is that they are reactions to populist uprisings, that they rely on demobilization rather than mobilization of their populations, and that they are propped by police and military coercion rather than hegemonic projects.

Returning to the issue of affects and symbols divided by the emptiness between them, we start to see the root of this asymmetry in the genesis of both post-Maidan and anti-Maidan type of regimes. The Maidan uprising, like the space-centric protests of the Occupy-type and the early Arab Spring before it, created an affective community consolidated by the experience of violence and common suffering. This affective community destroyed the symbolic landscape of the pax postsovietica without offering anything comparable in return. In reaction to this, the anti-Maidan movements and later regimes doubled down on asserting the symbolic remnants of the post-Soviet civilization, protecting the statues, flags, and steles. However, they also failed to offer a hegemonic project that would imbue the dead letter of such symbols with a new lifeworld.

17.05.2022
first published on *Emptiness*

Together We Stand: Enforced Single Motherhood and Ukrainian Refugees Care Networks

Oksana Dutchak

With the beginning of the Russian invasion of Ukraine in February 2022, approximately 7.8 million Ukrainians have fled to European countries[1], searching for safety abroad[2]. According to UNHCR Regional intentions report, approximately 87%[3] of Ukrainian refugees are women and children. Some recalculation of the report results allows an estimation of 35% or approximately 2.7 million Ukrainian children in Europe[4]. Due to the decision of the Ukrainian government to restrict men's cross-border mobility, this crossborder displacement is extremely gendered and leads to the reconfiguration of labor in separated families. The structures of gender and economic inequality have placed a disproportionate share of reproductive labor on women in all societies, including in Ukraine. However, in the case of Ukrainian refugees, it seems more appropriate to speak not about this disproportionate burden, but about the phenomenon of enforced single motherhood, where the entire responsibility of reproductive labor falls on women's shoulders.

In this article I analyze how reproductive labor is managed by Ukrainian refugees in the context of enforced single motherhood. I am particularly focused on the role that informal networks of support play. While being deeply gendered and depoliticized, these networks offer women a source of time, critically needed for social reproduction. How are these networks of support (re) created in and after displacement? How do they structure the lives and experiences of Ukrainian refugees? Which structures of inequalities stand behind them and how should these informal networks be evaluated from a political perspective? I will provide some preliminary answers, based on interviews with Ukrainian refugees, participatory observation and, well, my own experience of enforced single motherhood in refuge.

The private case of social reproduction under capitalism

The ideal model of capitalism presupposes that people earn money to sustain their life and the lives of their families. However, in the structures of socio-economic inequalities which lead to poverty wages and unemployment, society obviously cannot rely only on paid employment to get resources for social reproduction. Moreover, this ideal model ideologically and practically ignores the part of social reproduction that requires reproductive labor; namely housework and care labor, without which individuals, families, communities, capitalist production and society as a whole cannot function. This critique has been foregrounded by feminist Marxist theory of social reproduction[5].

While there are a lot of ongoing theoretical debates in Marxist theory of social reproduction, they go beyond the purpose of this article. But what is important in the context of everyday mechanics of social reproduction, as Marxist theory highlights, is that people attain additional resources for social reproduction from state intervention, charity, subsistence agriculture, and informal networks[6]. Hence, the puzzle of social reproduction in capitalist society is impossible to solve without paying attention to extra-market relations.

All in all, social reproduction in modern societies stands on the shaky (im)balance between material resources and time, upheld by structures of capitalism and patriarchy. On the one hand, material resources for social reproduction of the working classes are attained predominantly from paid work, which requires time to exercise one's labor power. These are supplemented by material resources from other activities, some of which also require time, like subsistence agriculture or side-jobs. To

Oksana Dutchak is a member of the editorial team of the *Commons*, PhD in social sciences. Research interests: protests, workers' protests, gender inequality, care labor, Marxism, Marxist feminism.

"get" that time, together with time for reproductive labor, other sources are used,[7] where state intervention and informal networks are the most stable and, hence, play the dominant role.

Unlike state intervention in the form of care infrastructure, informal networks stay behind the curtain of private life. Though their role is immense, it is also naturalized and depoliticized. In the context of war, displacement, and policies that enforce single motherhood among Ukrainian refugees, the role of informal networks becomes quite prominent. Though this role has always been considerable.

Stitching the gaps of care

Back in pre-war "normality," despite persistent gender inequality, Ukrainian women were integrated into the local (predominantly public) care system. This system, however, has been haunted by neoliberal austerity for years.[8] Presented as an "optimization" of kindergartens, schools, hospitals and other care facilities against the background of chronic underfinancing, reforms of care infrastructures created a feminized cohort of working poor[9] as well as recurring gaps in access to and functioning of care institutions,[10] thus deepening gender inequality.

As in other societies, the care gaps have been managed inside nuclear or extended families, channeled through personal networks of support and local communities. Being gendered and deeply personalized (creating yet another form of inequality; for example, for single mothers[11]), these networks of support have been stitching together the holes in the fabric of social reproduction. However, with the onset of war and displacement, women have been further deprived of support from care institutions and networks.

Displaced across the border and forced into single motherhood, Ukrainian refugees are often faced with the inability to fully integrate into local care institutions. This is due to both migration trends and structural problems in care institutions, such as the lack of capacities and workers, shorter working hours, etc. In many cases they are faced with the same care gaps, which have been created by the local variations of neoliberal austerity[12]. At the same time, Ukrainian refugees have to manage different additional tasks, related to bureaucracy, paid labor, health issues and their own integration into a hosting society.

All in all, dispersed along the lines of local specificity and differing policies in the hosting societies, Ukrainian refugees have to manage the gaps of local care institutions on their own. Alternatively, they can look for additional support either from volunteer initiatives or from traditional informal networks. However, the first option is sporadic and can provide women only with short-term and sometimes unpredictable assistance in reproductive labor. Volunteers and different organizations can care for their children at best several hours per week and their activities may easily vanish or have already vanished. And while traditional — in the sense of being accustomed to — informal networks often remain the only answer, being cut off from them so abruptly means that these networks do not flourish automatically. Though "spinning" (networking) skills and reciprocal usage of these networks are embedded in female gender roles and socialization, understanding of spinning circumstances and patterns highlights both how important they are and which structures of inequalities stand behind them.

Transferring and mobilizing networks of support

The most predictable strategy, used by Ukrainian refugees with children, is to flee the war together with friends and relatives in order to transfer the fragments of their existing support networks across the border. Due to governmental restrictions, mostly the female part of the women's networks are the one crossing the borders: mothers, sisters, and female friends. They often settle together or nearby and are more or less actively involved in domestic and care labor, supporting those in enforced single motherhood. This transfer and arrangements are relatively planned (though many decisions are made in a situation of emergency) and reproduce the accustomed patterns of care.

The most "natural" refugees' care arrangements which are transferred in this case involve women from a family's older generation. In Ukraine, as in many other societies, grandmothers often play an active role, sometimes becoming a child's primary caretaker, compensating for the lack of affordable options of childcare before the age of 3, or become the second carer in single mothers' households. Such a "natural" arrangement in Ukrainian society rests on structures of capitalist and patriarchal inequalities. On the one hand, due to low wages, many families cannot survive with one wage-earner while another adult (the mother of a child — in a vast majority of cases) is on childcare leave. This pushes both parents to the labor market and forces them to look for alternative care options.

Traditional gender roles, a relatively low pension age (60-65 years[13]), very low pensions (115 EUR on average[14]), discrimination against older women on the labor market and unaffordable housing which forces different generations to cohabitate — all are factors that make a grandmother the most common carer from one's own extended family. Fleeing with such *preexisting* networks and care arrangements is the most predictable and stable.

Other strategies involve the mobilization and partial spinning of the existing networks. First of all, the existing crossborder networks influence women's decisions regarding the destination to which to flee. In this case, destinations of the enforced single mothers are adjusted according to potential networks of support in host countries. As they flee, women will often choose to go to a country and a city where someone they know is already based there, and settle in their household or at least nearby in order to be able to access permanent or sporadic assistance with reproductive labor. Here all the possible networks can be involved, starting with close relatives and friends, and ending with relatively distant acquaintances.

For example, one woman, with whom I've talked, has chosen her destination because of her mother's female friend living nearby. Another was heading to a place where her ex-colleague was living with her family. In the end, this strategy can work or can fail in the sense that here we are not speaking about the actual, but about potential networks of support. Care arrangements can be negotiated in advance or they can be just assumed, but they can fail to work in both cases.

Network transfers can also go together with network spinning, when women flee the war together with those who have not provided active support in their care labor before, but agreed to do so. Sometimes these transfers take the shape of unaccustomed cooperation between different families with children, when loosely related families, without previous care arrangements, depart and settle together to support each other. Exchange of resources can happen within these cooperation arrangements. For example, one woman can provide time in the form of childcare for both her and another family's child, and get material support in return from that family.

These cooperative families can be related in different ways — as relatives, friends, acquaintances, neighbors and even colleagues. In other words, all possible types of networks can also be mobilized. In one case, a woman fled with her husband's friend and his family. In another, female colleagues with children decided to flee and settle together. There are cases when such cooperative departures are organized from the outside and pre-designed to provide mutual care arrangement.

In one case, a residence was organized for cultural workers with children, and they settled together and supported each other in care provision. In another case, a foreign corporation arranged the departure of its workers to a neighboring country and settled them in a hotel together. In the end, women continued to work at a local factory branch of this corporation and provided care for each other's children in shifts. Though the last arrangement helps women to deal with their double roles as single carers and workers, it also allows the corporation to deal with the situation without extra expenses. In this case, one can speak about the merging of the profit-oriented approach and an assumption about "natural" solutions, instead of socializing care.

Spinning the net of support

In many cases, though, when network transfer or mobilization is not possible, women in enforced single motherhood have to spin them from scratch. This spinning is often spatially localized where settlement and care labor are concentrated. Women refugees meet each other in camps and dormitories where they are accommodated, in long lines when managing paperwork and social payments, in kindergartens, schools and playgrounds, during events, and in social media or chat groups organized for Ukrainian refugees with children. These settings become nodes which facilitate mutual recognition and experiences, enabling, shortening and simplifying precisely the type of connections where reciprocity of care assistance can emerge.

The degree of mutual care can greatly vary in the newly created networks and depends both on women's needs for assistance and their capacities to provide them in return. For example, in an extreme but not a very common case, a woman with a toddler who cannot find a place in local kindergartens but still has or wants to go to integration courses, looks for another woman in the same situation to babysit in shifts. Such announcements appeared from time to time in local support chats, though, it is hard to say to which extent this type of arrangement works. I have not come across such functional cases, and one woman with whom I've talked was complaining that she tried to organize a similar exchange but did not receive a positive response from other refugee women.

For those whose children are in primary schools, the schoolyard becomes the place of meeting and building initial connections which can evolve into networks of support — this is especially facilitated in cases when separate classes for Ukrainian children are created. It is quite common that women who live nearby pick up children from school in turns. This can be both as a regular practice, as well as a way to deal with emergencies, when for some reason a mother cannot make it. The older the children, the less care support women need. Refugees with teenagers use newly created networks rather for other purposes: psychological support, information exchange, socialization, etc.

When in the same situation, sharing the same experience and having opportunities to meet and connect in spaces explicitly related to social reproduction, Ukrainian refugees tend to support each other in care. However, gender roles and gender socialization can lead to solidarity networks outside of this community. There are stories when women were helped by hosting families — not only in terms of settling, but also sporadically in managing care. One woman said that in her case the main support in care labor came from a female neighbor from Turkey. Having children herself, and knowing what it meant to be with them in a foreign country, the neighbor proposed to look after the Ukrainian refugee's child so her mother could have some time to care for herself.

The lack of support networks and how this influences women in refuge is another side of the story. From my conversations with Ukrainian refugees it becomes obvious that the lack of support and the inability to find and establish a care network can lead to an inability to manage in enforced single motherhood, both physically and psychologically, and sometimes even to choose to return with one's children back to Ukraine. Though this experience is harder to track, it appears that a fear of detachment from one's usual networks of support may also play a great role for those who decide to stay with their children in their hometowns or to flee only inside the country, still facing the threat of shelling, power cuts, lack of income, and a harsh winter.

Their Political Future and the Structures Behind Refugees' Care Networks

Displacement, triggered by Russian military aggression and border regulations, shaped by the Ukrainian government, influence the initial pool of networks which can be transferred, mobilized, and created to manage enforced single motherhood. However, in most cases the care part of refugee support is centered on female figures: female relatives, friends, colleagues, and acquaintances. Structures of gender and economic inequalities, gender roles and socialization, naturalize women as carers and the ones responsible for unpaid reproductive labor. This explains the gendered character of previously established, negotiated, assumed and newly created care arrangements for women escaping the war. Predominantly female networks of support have been used in Ukraine before the war, as in many other countries, to stitch the gaps created by profit-oriented economies and austerity-driven policies. This continues in the refuge.

The structures of class and income inequality may also play a paradoxical role in refugees' access to care networks. Those women, who are otherwise in a more privileged position due to available income and previously established professional connections abroad, often settle immediately or quite fast in a separate apartment and don't need social payments. While this makes the material side of their life far easier, it also partially cuts them off from other Ukrainian refugees: they don't cohabit in camps and dormitories, they don't have to go regularly to different social institutions. In the end, they may have far less possibilities to build connections and create a network of care. One woman, who had lived for five months in a camp with her toddler and then was settled in a dormitory, cohabiting with another family, said she was lucky: unlike her sister, who settled in a separate apartment, she could build connections with other Ukrainian women who could support her in care. Another woman, who works in a research institution and lives separately with her son, said explicitly that she felt isolated and there was nobody to back her up.

The described networks of support are definitely about everyday solidarity and reciprocity. However, this solidarity is not necessarily translated into organized collective efforts to deal with the problems of social reproduction and structural inequalities which create them. Situated in the sphere of reproduction, artificially pushed into the private sphere in modern societies, relying on and spinning around naturalized care work, female networks of everyday solidarity and reciprocity have only a very basic potentiality for political mobilization.

Refugees' care networks are additionally fragmented and fluid; they bear the burden of vulnerability, rooted in the situation of war and displacement. Nevertheless, sometimes these networks are used to mobilize Ukrainian refugees in volunteering or political efforts to deal with the war and its consequences: information about protest events in support of Ukraine, or collective efforts needed for humanitarian or military support is circulating there. In this respect they currently play the role of supplementary networks, vaguely centered around different political or cause-oriented initiatives. To which extent these networks can be mobilized to deal with the problems of care infrastructure on the level of policies — either in refuge or back in Ukraine — remains an open question.

Footnotes

[1] UNHCR. November 2022. "Operational Data Portal: Ukrainian refugee situation." https://data.unhcr.org/en/situations/ukraine.

[2] Out of 7.8 million, 4.7 million registered for Temporary Protection or similar national protection schemes in Europe. Additionally, 2.8 million are reported in Russia and from tens of thousand to over one hundred thousand in different non-EU countries.

[3] UNHCR. September 2022. "Lives on Hold: Intentions and Perspectives of Refugees from Ukraine #2". https://data.unhcr.org/en/documents/details/95767.

[4] According to UNHCR report, children 0-17 years old constitute 35% of refugees' households.

[5] Bakker, Isabella, and Rachel Silvey. "Introduction: Social reproduction and global transformations–from the everyday to the global." Beyond states and markets: The challenges of social reproduction (2008): 1-15; Katz, Cindi. "Vagabond capitalism and the necessity of social reproduction." Antipode 33.4 (2001): 709-728; Ferguson, Susan, and David McNally. "Capital, Labour-Power, and Gender-Relations: Introduction to the Historical Materialism Edition of Marxism and the Oppression of Women." Marxism and the Oppression of Women. London: Brill (2013); Federici, Silvia. "On Primitive Accumulation, Globalization and Reproduction." Friktion: Magasin for køn, krop, and kultur (2017); And others.

[6] Gimenez, Martha E. "Capitalism and the oppression of women: Marx revisited." Science & Society (2005): 11-32; Mies, Maria. "Patriarchy and accumulation on a world scale revisited. (Keynote lecture at the Green Economics Institute, Reading, 29 October 2005)." International Journal of Green Economics 1.3-4 (2007): 268-275; Rioux, Sébastien. "Embodied contradictions: Capitalism, social reproduction and body formation." Women's Studies International Forum. Vol. 48. Pergamon, 2015; And others.

[7] Dutchak, Oksana. 2018. "Conditions and Sources of Labor Reproduction in Global Supply Chains: the Case of Ukrainian Garment Sector". Pp. 19-26 In Bulletin of Taras Shevchenko National University of Kyiv. Sociology, # 9.

[8] Dutchak, Oksana. 2018. "Crisis, War and Austerity: Devaluation of Female Labor and Retreating of the State". Rosa Luxemburg Stiftung, Berlin.

[9] Tkalich, Olena. 2020. ""Be like Nina": how the movement of nurses was born during the pandemic and health care reform". Commons [in Ukrainian] https://commons.com.ua/uk/ruh-medsester-pid-chas-medreformy-i-pandemii/.

[10] Dutchak, Oksana, Olena Strelnyk, Olena Tkalich. 2020. "Who cares? Kindergartens in the context of gender inequality". Center for Social and Labor Research, Kyiv; and Dutchak, Oksana. 2021. "They Will 'Manage Somehow': Notes from Ukraine on Care Labor in the Time of the Local and Global Crises". Pp. 105-112 in Essential Struggles: Pandemic Fronts. LevFem, Friedrich-Ebert-Stiftung, Sofia.

[11] Dutchak, Oksana, Olena Tkalich. 2021. "Single mothers in Ukraine. Poverty, violation of rights and protest potential". Commons [in Ukrainian] https://commons.com.ua/uk/odinoki-materi-v-ukrayini-bidnist-porushennya-prav-ta-potencial-do-protestu/.

[12] Of course, the diversity of policies, resources and capacities of the European care infrastructure is huge. This influences the experiences of Ukrainian refugees greatly and in many cases they find themselves in the care and social systems which function far better than a Ukrainian one before the war. However, in all cases some varying share of reproductive labor is left behind and this variety is shaped by the scope and dynamics of austerity policies in every country.

[13] Depending on the duration of working experience: if the working experience is 29 years and more, a person can retire being 60 years old; with working experience 15-19 years one must be 65 to retire. Before the pension reform, initiated in 2011, the pension age was 55 years for women and 60 years for men. There are plans to increase the pension age further.

[14] As of July 2022, there were 10.8 million retired people in Ukraine. The average pension was UAH 4437 (EUR 115). Approximately 43% of retired people in

Ukraine were getting below UAH 3000 (EUR 78). On average women are getting 30% lower pensions than men.

18.01.2023
first published on *LEFTEAST*

The material was published as part of a special project organized by the *Eastern European Left Media Outlet* and dedicated to the topic of transnational migration in the countries of Central and Eastern Europe.

52 Apartments for Internally Displaced People: The Gap between Housing Policy and the Shocks of War

Alona Liasheva

The full-scale Russian invasion of Ukraine caused an unprecedented housing crisis. More than hundred thousand homes have been destroyed or damaged, and millions of Ukrainians have had to flee. Ukrainian housing policy has not managed to adequately address the housing needs of internally displaced people (IDPs), though some civil society organizations and municipal urban administrations have created new non-profit forms of tenancy to aid IDPs. Yet, the situation in Ukraine still remains critical and necessitates a careful rethinking of the goals and mechanisms of housing policy in order to reshape the housing system in accordance with the new, wartime needs of Ukrainians.

The new housing crisis

The full-scale Russian invasion brought an unprecedented level of destruction and displacement. Conditions differ widely by family and individual. Some were able to return to their homes in Kyiv after the area was liberated, while others still cannot escape occupied Mariupol' where their homes have been destroyed. Future Ukrainian housing policy will have to grapple with this diverse and changing situation on the ground. In this paper I offer the following classification system for displacement: 1. displacement caused by the dangers of war; 2. displacement caused by the destruction of homes; and 3. displacement caused by the rental market itself.

The first category of displaced people is by far the largest. The majority of displaced people in Ukraine left their homes to escape imminent danger to their life and health, an occupying regime, and the serious humanitarian crisis brought on by the invasion. In August 2022 the UN Refugee Agency estimated that there are 6,865,625 refugees from Ukraine in Europe and 6,645,000 IDPs in Ukraine. The majority of IDPs and refugees still have their homes and some are already coming back or planning to come back when the situation is safer, while some are willing to stay in the places they moved to.

Many, however, have no home to return to. This second category of displaced people are in a much more unstable situation, as their ability to get decent housing in the short term is far lower. According to Olena Shuliak, the Deputy Head of the Committee of the Verkhovna Rada, 15 million square meters of housing has been destroyed by the Russian army and nearly 800.000 Ukrainians have lost their homes due to the war. The most affected oblasts are Donetsk, Kharkiv, Kyiv, and Chernihiv. 220.000 people have already applied for compensation for destroyed housing. These people need to be temporarily housed while their homes are being rebuilt or repaired. Also, it is very probable that a significant number of them might not be willing to return to the place they used to live.

The third category of displaced people receives much less attention: tenants displaced due to the sky-rocketing prices in the rental market in the western regions of Ukraine. Transparency International states that between October 2021 and May 2022 the rents in the Lviv region increased by 96%, in the Uzhgorod region by 225%, and in Ivano-Frankivsk by 128%. Since then the price increases have calmed down slightly, but rent remains unaffordable not only for IDPs but also for locals. Landlords in these regions evicted many of their previous tenants in order to rent to IDPs from war torn regions who were willing to pay double the price, resulting in a highly speculative rental market. As the Ukrainian rental market

Alona Liasheva is a member of the editorial team of the *Commons*, sociologist, researcher of urban political economy. Now she's doing research on war everyday life and Ukrainian resistance.

is predominantly informal, there is no way to estimate the number of such evictions.

Housing before and during the war

Though accentuated sharply by the Russian invasion, the Ukrainian housing crisis has deep roots. During the Soviet period, housing in Ukraine was predominantly produced and redistributed by the state, though this redistribution was uneven and benefited the part of the working class that was deemed 'useful'. Following the collapse of the Soviet Union and the transition to a market economy, Ukrainian housing policy has centered on homeownership as the main way of providing housing. This was done through: the mass privatization of housing in the 1990s; state support for the mortgage market in the 2000s; state support for private developers, especially through land-use policy; state subsidies to buy housing; a mass disinvestment in public housing; and the total absence of efficient regulations for the rental market.

With the Russian annexation of Crimea and the start of the war in the Donbas in 2014, around a million and a half of Ukrainians fled the occupied territories and territories along the front line. Finding housing for these IDPs suddenly became a key issue in Ukraine. Initial state efforts to provide housing during this crisis sought to aid displaced individuals in buying their own private flats. But such programs ended up providing only several hundred private flats a year. As a result, in 2020, after 6 years of war, approximately 70% of IDPs still had not found adequate housing. The goal of providing each family with a privately owned home proved impossible, even when the state channeled more funds into these programs. At the same time, the state provided social housing on an extremely low level (only around 1500 flats, the majority of which were in eastern Ukraine and are now lost). The rental market also remained unregulated, leaving IDPs on their own, many of whom faced discrimination from landlords both due to economic factors and to prejudice against people from Donbas.

This experience was repeated after the full-scale Russian invasion, though this time was far more catastrophic. In the first month, the Ukrainian state only managed to provide temporary housing for some IDPs. Most of this temporary housing is student dormitories and module housing. Such options are neither comfortable nor long-term. They need to be replaced with more sustainable housing, where you can have a home, not just a bed to sleep in and a roof above your head. Still the only long-term solution offered by the state is for IDPs to buy housing with low-rate mortgages. We have already seen how such programs didn't work in the aftermath of 2014. The Ukrainian state still has made no effort to meet the actual needs of displaced people through regulation of the rental market, placing a hold on evictions, or providing any kind of non-profit housing. Since the full-scale invasion, the state's main housing institution, the State Fund for Support of Youth Housing Construction, has bought only 52 flats for 6-7 million IDPs.

How have IDPs managed to survive?

In March and April of 2022 together with a group of colleagues I collected interviews with non-combatants, both people who had left their homes and arrived in western Ukraine and locals who had witnessed the mass influx of IDPs. This data reveals various ways in which people managed to house themselves and demonstrates how networks of civil society and local government have reacted to the crisis. It also points out the problems of profit-oriented housing policy in Ukraine.

The first practice applied by local authorities was to provide temporary housing. Temporary shelters were organized in municipal facilities such as schools and sporthalls. Due to the COVID-19 pandemic educational spaces were not in use, thus they became the public resource mobilized for temporary housing. The same process occurred in the private and civil sectors with the offices of companies and NGOs and cultural spaces being turned into shelters. These were predominantly self-organized efforts, however, much depended on infrastructural resources available before the escalation of the war. Municipalities managed to provide the infrastructure, but the management of displaced people was done by volunteers. Ultimately much of this temporary housing ended up becoming long-term, as greedy landlords in Western Ukraine set exorbitant rates for rent that few IDPs could meet.

Also the absence of social housing programs and social housing units contributed to the growing housing crisis, the only exception being a few uncoordinated decisions by regional, urban, or university authorities to use available housing as non-profit housing. In some places, like Vinnytsia, municipal institutions have been set up to negotiate between IDPs and landlords, limiting rental speculation, evictions, and discrimination against renters. Such policies are emergency crisis measures, but they could potentially become the basis for socially-oriented housing policy. However, the chances of putting such policies into practice on a mass scale is very low, as Ukrainian state housing policy remains oriented towards subsidizing private homeownership. Current state programs for displaced people are intended to invest both in the supply and the demand side of the housing development, an approach which, aside from being completely ineffective, supports the developers, not the people.

The Ukrainian state and international partners' plans for 'Rebuilding Ukraine'

As a response to the massive destruction of housing and infrastructure, the Ukrainian government is designing the so-called 'Rebuilding Ukraine' plan, of which housing policy is a key component. On the international level, the financing of the 'Rebuilding' will affect not only the housing sector but the structure of the Ukrainian economy for the following years or even decades. At the moment, Ukraine expects inflow of liquidity from international financial institutions, such as the IMF, from partner states, and from reparations in the form of confiscated Russian assets in the West. Such aid is being planned in the form of grants and credits. While Ukrainian foreign debt is not being restructured, these credits will deepen the Ukrainian economy's dependence on foreign financial institutions, making investment in non-profit housing more difficult. On the national level, the internal distribution of this foreign aid will only perpetuate the existing housing policy that supports homeownership and ignores non-profit housing.

What kind of housing policy does Ukraine need?

Housing or any other kind of social policy should be based on people's needs. Huge numbers of Ukrainians have had to flee. For many this displacement is temporary, for others long-term, and for some it will become permanent. Some have no home to return to. Even some of those who didn't have to flee have been evicted because of the skyrocketing rent market. Ukrainian IDPs' futures depend not only on the development of war, but also the possibilities of employment, old and new social contacts, and a feeling of belonging in one's home that may be broken. That's why the housing sector should be more diverse, so it can adjust to various and changing needs.

Effective regulation of the rental market and the creation of decent, non-profit housing has the capacity to help solve not only the housing crisis caused by war and benefit post-war recovery, but also save lives during the war and even help Ukraine to win. Here the history of housing policy during and after the First and Second World Wars can offer solutions in the present..

The regulation of the rental market became widespread during WWI, when militaries, refugees, and many other social groups were in great need of social support. Following the example of France, most European countries, their colonies, the Russian Empire, and certain regions of the US placed a moratorium on rent and evictions from 1914 till 1920. Such policies helped displaced people find housing in safe regions and stay there, while at the same time providing militaries with housing near the front. WWII brought on a much larger wave of social housing policy in Europe. This type of policy helped poor people, refugees, and the families of the military not to end up on the streets or in the line of fire.

After almost a year since the full-scale invasion of Ukraine by Russia, the limited attempts by several municipal officials to regulate the rental market in certain Ukrainian cities has not led to any palpable results due to lack of support from the national government, especially from the MinRegion, which is responsible for housing policy. Most Ukrainian IDPs still live in uncomfortable, temporary shelters or have had to return to cities still suffering from Russian shelling.

The development of a non-profit rental sector can already right now make housing more affordable and provide housing to those who need it most much faster than the process of rebuilding and compensation currently being proposed by the Ukrainian government. This non-profit housing could be organized by municipalities and state companies as much as through private developers, ensuring that a portion of the housing stock is collectively owned.

The Russian invasion in February has caused a housing crisis that is spiraling out of control, though housing activists have been strengthening their efforts and a grassroots movement to create affordable housing is growing. These activists seek to regulate the rental market and implement both social and cooperative housing. For example, housing activists from Lviv demand the concession of vacant buildings for the use as temporary housing for IDPs. A collective of IDPs has been working since the start of the war to build cooperative housing themselves. Such initiatives involve networking, the sharing of experience, involve local government, and make demands on the national government.

In such an apocalyptic times Ukrainian society has a chance to fight and obtain the right for decent housing. The voices of Ukrainians demanding such rights must be included in the rebuilding process to ensure decent living conditions in the decades that will follow the war.

For the millions of IDPs and Ukrainians simply facing rampant housing insecurity, this crisis offers an opportunity to reform the Ukrainian housing sector around the needs of the people, not the developers and landlords.

23.09.2022
edited version

The Far Right in Ukraine
Interview with Taras Bilous

Interviewed by Stephen R. Shalom,

a member of the *New Politics* editorial board.

Translated by **Denys Pilash**

New Politics (NP): *How would you assess the influence of far-right forces in Ukraine? We have seen claims that, on the one hand, suggest that Ukraine is a Nazi state, or, on the other hand, that the far right is an insignificant factor in Ukrainian life. What is your assessment?*

Taras Bilous (TB): Basically, their electoral influence is abysmal, it is small, but they use their strengths in other fields, like on the streets, to try to influence policies. Their extra-parliamentary influence should be neither diminished nor exaggerated.

NP: *Is it the case that the far right has the ability to block policies it doesn't like by threatening violence?*

TB: The most significant example of this was the so-called "protest against capitulation," the protest against peace initiatives in late 2019 after Zelensky was elected president. This was an effort by the nationalist right to stop the initiation of the peace process. There had been an agreement that there would be a troop disengagement at three points of what was then the line between Ukrainian forces and Russian/separatist forces in Donbas. Then people from around the Azov movement, and from the National Corps Party, staged a campaign there, at one of these points, presenting this disengagement as if it represented some kind of gain for the Kremlin, as if Ukrainian troops alone were called upon to withdraw and leave their positions. But this wasn't what the disengagement required; it required both sides to pull back.

But even in this case, which was so crucial for the right, where they tried to achieve their maximum mobilization for this activity, they didn't succeed in achieving their point of view because Zelensky intervened person-ally. He traveled to that line of forces and engaged in heated discussions with some Azov members, and eventually Ukraine did carry out this disengagement, which was a prerequisite for resuming the meeting in the "Normandy Format" with France and Germany as mediators between Ukraine and Russia. So even in this case the right was unable to block governmental policy.

It's not only a matter of how much effort the far right puts into their campaigns that determines whether they succeed. It's especially a question of how their positions align with the broader position of Ukrainian society in general, because when their demands contradict the position of the majority of the society, it's much harder for them to push them through; on the other hand, when they support the position of the broader population, then they have more chance of influencing government decisions.

Some of the Western leftist press made it seem as if Zelensky retreated on his policies under the pressure of the far right. But they didn't succeed in thwarting his peace initiatives, which were favored by the majority of the Ukrainian population and for which Zelensky felt he had a popular mandate. On the other hand, the polls showed that the majority of Ukrainians, while supporting the peace process, rejected some specific political demands pushed by the Russian side. And here Zelensky had to backtrack.

In those policy areas where the positions of the far right did not coincide with the views of liberals and national liberals, the far right wasn't successful in fulfilling their pressure on the government. For instance, on gender policies or LGBTQ issues, where the right found itself in the minority, it wasn't able to influence governmental decisions

NP: Could you say a bit more about the behavior of the far right towards feminists and LGBTQ people? And what is the role of the Ukrainian police and security forces in dealing with this?

TB: Far-right groups before the war actively tried to disrupt different events promoting women's and LGBTQ rights. Here we could see that the reaction of the State and the police was heavily dependent on whether the event had a lot of international coverage, like for instance, the Pride parade in Kyiv or the 8th of March women's demos. In which case the authorities and the police tried to prevent these far-right attacks. However, at lesser-known events in the provinces, in some smaller cities and towns, they were also actively attacked by the far right, and then the police were usually quite inactive, standing by and doing nothing. So in these cases the far right was more successful in attacking and disrupting these events.

There was a general phenomenon of the far right infiltrating the security services and law enforcement, but it's hard to measure to what extent this occurred. We know some prime examples, for instance, the local head of the Kyiv police came from an Azov background. When we had confrontations between leftist and far-right activists, we often saw the police greeting some from the far right, showing that they were familiar with each other. This again implied that there were some connections. But actually it seems that this wasn't so widespread.

Even in those cases where the police do nothing to prevent attacks on feminist and other progressive events, it doesn't automatically mean that they do this because they feel affinity for the attackers or that they have some connections to them. The police are not doing their pri-

mary job, which is to protect peaceful gatherings, but not so much because they are on the side of attacks, but because abstaining and doing nothing cause them fewer problems. Defending an LGBT event (for example) can lead to far-right attacks on the police, which can lead to police injuries. Therefore, to avoid a fight with the far right, it is easier for them to simply do nothing. The arrest of the far right will lead to other far-right mobilizing, organizing a picket outside the police station, and generally putting pressure on the police. The police want less trouble, so it's often easier for them to insist that the organizers cancel their event, than to fight the far right. Of course, this is the failure of the police to fulfill its duty to protect freedom of assembly. They behave similarly in cases of conflicts with high-ranking officials or other persons who may create problems for them.

The situation was improving, however, after the removal of Interior Minister Arsen Avakov, who was widely seen as a patron of the National Corps and other far-right groups. After he left office in 2021, there was a series of arrests of far-right activists, and we could feel a general improvement in the situation, and there were trends showing that far-right influence in the security services was shrinking.

But the situation might be different in the case of the so-called municipal guards. These are paramilitary structures that were created in some cities as assistants to police law enforcement, in many cases with rather dubious legal status. The far right tried to present this as a way to employ veterans of the war.

The far right infiltrated the municipal guard in Kyiv and some other places, and actually played major roles. They were accountable to the local authorities, to the municipal leadership, to the mayors, but at the same time they had this very questionable legal status. So this was an opportunity for the far right to gain more influence. In other cities, though, the far right wasn't present in creating the municipal guards. Instead they were usually comprised of some kind of athletes and were just loyal servants to the local elites, almost in a feudal way.

NP: What was the relationship between the Ukrainian left and the Ukrainian far right before the war?

TB: Well, obviously, our attitude was directly opposed to them, and we were in perpetual confrontation with them. But we can say that the war in Donbas, when it started in 2014, contributed to the decline of the strength of leftist movements, and in the streets the far right grew more powerful, while the left was in decline. Actually in these confrontations with the far right, the best outcome was usually a draw. But in recent years there was some reversal of these trends, and there was a revival of the street antifa movement and some anti-fascist victories on the side of the left. So there were some signs that the situation was reversing direction.

NP: Turning to February 2022, how has the full-scale war affected the influence of the far right?

TB: It is not an easy task to answer this question, because with the war political life in Ukraine has been put on pause. It's quite complicated to predict what the situation will be after the war given that it's so dependent on the war's outcome.

So what changed with the war? Lots of the far right, the majority of them, went into the military. Some remained, and sometimes they did some controversial things behind the lines — but they were usually criticized for this by general public opinion. So, for instance, when the far right did its usual stuff and tried to attack and discredit a feminist protest in Lviv against domestic violence, it actually rather backfired because they didn't find some huge popular support for the activity. On the contrary, the coverage was favorable to the feminist activists and to supporting organizations, including ours, including from one popular YouTube blogger, and in some mainstream media. So we can say that far-right activity of this sort isn't very much tolerated behind the lines.

This is actually very important, because it was precisely the weakness of resistance to the far right, the uncritical attitude towards them in the mainstream media and from a significant part of the moderate public, that was one of the main advantages of the Ukrainian far right. They skillfully used the halo of "heroes" they had won on the Maidan in 2014 and in the war in Donbas to protect themselves from criticism.

In fact, if you evaluate the power of the Ukrainian far right in absolute terms, it has never set a record. Everyone knows about their electoral weakness, but even if we talk about street mobilizations, the Polish far right is definitely stronger than their Ukrainian "colleagues" in this regard. It's enough to compare each year the largest street marches — October 14 in Ukraine and November 11 in Poland — to understand this. In terms of the scale of violence, the Ukrainian far right also pales in comparison to what the Russian far right did in the 2000s, often under the cover of the Russian special services. In fact, Ukrainian neo-Nazis acted before the Maidan in the shadow and under the great influence of Russian neo-Nazis. The main difference in the Ukrainian situation after the Maidan is not in the absolute power of the far right, but in its relative power compared to other political actors, as well as in the uncritical attitude of the mainstream moderate public towards them.

But in recent years, public opinion about them has changed, and this was one of the reasons why the anti-racist and anti-fascist antifa group Arsenal (Kyiv) dared to come out of the deep underground and challenge the far right again. In 2014-2018, in the case of clashes between the left and the right, public opinion was not on our side. But during the struggle in the summer of 2021, the far right became the "bad guys" in the media. And it seems that after the war this trend will continue because the far right will no longer be able to defend themselves from criticism as before.

NP: But why won't their war-time heroism, for example at Mariupol, enable them to deflect criticisms?

TB: It protects them. But only as a military unit. This does not transfer to the far right as a political actor.

Over the past years, Ukrainian society has come a long way in establishing the position that heroism at the front cannot be an indulgence for those who commit crimes and human rights violations in the rear. And although on some other issues during the full-scale war there was a worsening of the situation, on this issue I do not see a rollback.

Also, after this war, there will be veterans from all sectors of the population and on both sides of political conflicts. Now there are military volunteers even among the Roma, the most discriminated-against group in Ukrainian society — despite the fact that participation in the war goes against their own traditions. If in 2018 the far right managed to stage a series of pogroms against Roma without serious consequences for themselves, now this will no longer be the case.

But there is one category of people who will not be able to protect themselves in this way — the pro-Russian residents of Donbas and Crimea. Therefore, it is necessary that international organizations take an active part in the protection of human rights in these territories.

NP: Let's turn to the question of the Azov regiment. How significant are they? Are they an independent military force? Do they have their own far-right symbols? And, to ask about an issue that's been raised on the US left, is US military aid to Ukraine actually arming neo-Nazi units?

TB: The Azov regiment was integrated inside the National Guard and inside the official structures, but it still retained some level of autonomy. There were some steps to control it by Ukrainian officials, like to change its leadership, but it still retained its links with its founders like Andriy Biletsky, and it even had its own Sergeant School.

The majority of original Azov regiment were in Mariupol, and lots of them were taken prisoner. Some were exchanged in prisoner swaps, but the majority are still in in Russian captivity, and the commanders are interned in Turkey. Nevertheless, the regiment has been replenished with new people and continues recruiting. I don't know how much they managed to restore the structure.

What is more important after the full-scale invasion, the people associated with the Azov movement also set up a number of other units, like territorial defense units, for instance, which were connected to the Azov movement, using the Azov brand. The largest of them, the Kyiv Azov Special Operations Forces unit, was turned into an assault brigade at the end of January. So in general, compared to 2014 or 2021, in absolute numbers now far more far-right individuals have joined the military, and far more people are serving in the units they created. But at the same time, in relative terms, they play a smaller role in the war than in 2014, because the army in general has grown and modernized much more.

But it's important to understand that not only far-right individuals serve in the units created by the far right. (On the other hand, you can also find the far right in "regular" units). It's difficult to determine the percentages, but apolitical or centrist people often serve in far-right units, motivated by the high level of training and discipline in these units. When you join a fighting army, you first think about your chances of survival, the conditions of service, the competence of the officers, and the reliability of your fellow soldiers. Political views recede into the background. What will happen to these units and the people who serve in them after the war depends on the results of the war and the general political situation in Ukraine.

What I see with my own eyes is that the situation today is not comparable with 2014. Back then the level of State control over the military units that were created was minimal. Everything was very chaotic. I even know the story of how in 2014 one volunteer stole an entire armored personnel carrier and took it from Donbas to Western Ukraine. Today, however, there is strict control over the distribution of weapons, more control over these separate units, and from what I know, none of the recently founded smaller units enjoys a level of autonomy comparable with Azov in previous years. So actually, the situation is qualitatively quite different from what it was eight or nine years ago.

To illustrate this stricter state control over military units and over arms distribution, let me refer to my own experience. My previous battalion was disbanded, and I was transferred to some other one in our brigade. When the battalion was disbanded, it was discovered that several Kalashnikovs were missing. This triggered an immediate reaction from law enforcement. The military prosecutors office started an investigation and opened criminal cases against the officers who were responsible for the control of weapons in that battalion. This shows that the State tries to control very strictly where all the armaments and equipment goes, and that it's not going to some unauthorized individuals. This is one of aspect of the stricter state control over different armed units.

Regarding this notion of the West arming Nazis, and so on, the weapons are distributed more or less evenly among different units. So there might be some far-right people, people with far-right beliefs, in some units, but they are not specifically given this weaponry. Moreover, given the stricter control I described, this means that the weapons are going to be confiscated after the war, taken back by the State.

So more or less all the people who joined the armed forces are more or less equal in their access to different weapons. And obviously it's not the case that heavy weaponry from the West is being directed to far-right units. It's that ordinary units are getting the weapons, and maybe they have some people with far-right views, as well as people with all other beliefs, in their ranks. So there's no specific arming of the right.

Regarding the right-wing symbols, back in 2015, under pressure from the authorities, Azov removed the Black Sun from its insignia and tipped the emblem at an angle to distance itself from the far-right symbols. Last year, the departure from far-right symbols continued — the newly created Azov units use three swords instead of the symbol of the Azov regiment. The new brigade uses a symbol created on the basis of the previous emblem, but it has almost no resemblance to the Wolfsangel.

On the other hand, in the army now many soldiers and even lower-ranking officers wear various non-statutory military patches. It's a popular kind of merch that people buy at the military shops, it's not controlled in any way. They are often humorous, or have inscriptions on them like "Russian warship, go fuck yourself." But sometimes there are far-right symbols on these patches, like the Wolfsangel or Totenkopf. I have encountered cases where people wore patches with far-right symbols but had absolutely no understanding of its origin and meaning. One guy took off the Black Sun symbol when an anarchist from my former unit explained to him what it signified and showed him the Wikipedia article. Of course, those who started using these symbols in Ukraine understood well what they meant. But now if you see a guy with a Totenkopf, he might think it's just a skull and bones. So just because people use such symbols doesn't indicate that people are supporting their far-right meaning.

NP: Volodymyr Ishchenko, in a recent article in New Left Review, has argued that Ukraine in wartime, unlike other anti-colonial struggles, has become increasingly neoliberal, not more democratic, not more state interventionist, and not less corrupt. Do you think he is correct, and are these indications of the growing strength of the far right?

TB: Starting with the latter question, I don't see any relevance of the far right to this question. But regarding the first question, there are two separate aspects: one is about anti-democratic and authoritarian tendencies and the other is about social and economic policies. Regarding anti-democratic trends, actually we can't say that all previous national liberation movements were immune to that. On the contrary, war usually evokes more authoritarian and less democratic tendencies, and this applied to many of the liberation movements in Asia and Africa, just dictated by conditions. So, yes, obviously the war creates possibilities for authoritarian trends, and it can be used by the State authorities, by the government. But whether this will lead to more authoritarianism will heavily depend on the course and outcome of the war. And it's unclear how the far right will react to this, whether they will, in a way, try to adapt to this, to support it, or whether they will, on the contrary, fall victim to confrontation with the government. So actually there's a lot that is unspecified, due to the unclear outcome of the war.

Regarding social and the economic policies, again, we can't say that we have a clear picture, because on the one hand you have neo-liberal mantras and the liberalization of labor relations and labor markets. But on the other hand, there are objective reasons that push the Ukrainian Government — even though it speaks about privatization — to have undertaken a number of nationalizations in strategic sectors, nationalizing some big enterprises, factories that link to the military, to the energy sector, and so on. In addition, in the course of postwar reconstruction funds will be distributed via the State. So the percentage of the GDP that is concentrated in the hands of the State will clearly rise, both because of these nationalizations and the control of the reconstruction funds. So we cannot say that there is some very clear and one-sided tendency.

I have a thread on twitter about the class nature of the Zelensky government and I argue that it represents primarily the interests of middle bourgeoisie, or the classic bourgeoisie as opposed to both the working class and oligarchic capital. So on the one hand they are very eager and highly active in pushing neoliberal anti-labor legislation. But at the same time they are also interested in subduing the power of the oligarchs. Actually the war has already disrupted the level of oligarchic influence. So again, the outcome of the war will heavily influence both politics and the economy. And despite their neo-liberal ideology, they have been forced to carry out some steps that are contrary to their ideological positions in order to create a war economy.

NP: Finally, I'd like to ask you this. There is broad support in Ukraine for resisting the Russian invasion, from left to right. But in what ways does the left position on the war differ from that of the right in terms of goals and strategy?

TB: There are some pretty obvious distinctions in our and their visions of the future of postwar Ukraine. Obviously, the left wants a more socially-oriented, more pluralistic, more democratic, more inclusive country, while the far right, libertarians, and conservatives, stand for some opposite positions.

And then we have the question of self-determination, and it becomes a bit more complicated. When we go on to consider the issues of Crimea and Donbas, in the left camp there isn't a single position, but a spectrum of visions. We also do not have a consensus on the European Union and NATO.

The full-scale Russian invasion partially smoothed over the former conflicts between the various leftists in Ukraine, because on the most important issue, the absolute majority of the Ukrainian left took the same position — support and participation in the resistance. But the issues that divided the Ukrainian left in the past still haven't disappeared.

08.02.2023
first published on *New Politics*

For a Just Reconstruction

To Help Ukraine, Cancel Its Foreign Debt Interview with Oleksandr Kravchuk

Interviewed by David Broder

David Broder is *Jacobin*'s Europe editor and a historian of French and Italian communism. asked him about the country's economic situation and why debt cancellation is important if Ukrainians are to be able to shape their future.

In recent days, numerous governments have announced financial as well as military support for Ukraine, as it faces a devastating Russian invasion and an exodus of refugees already counting well over 1.5 million.

Such reliance on outside help is not new. Since the 1990s Ukraine's economy has lagged badly behind other former Eastern bloc countries, and — under the effects of global crisis, the pandemic and the war ongoing since 2014 — it has repeatedly turned to loans from the International Monetary Fund (IMF) and European Commission. Yet this lending was far from just altruism. Servicing the debt became an ever bigger share of public spending, and the loans also came on condition of specific policies designed to foster a "better business environment" and cut back the residual welfare state.

As Elliot Dolan-Evans notes at OpenDemocracy, even the European Commission's announcement of €1.2 billion support for Ukraine on February 21, just before the invasion, referred to unspecified "structural policy measures" in exchange for loans. Now, Ukrainian activists are calling for the cancellation of Ukraine's foreign debts. Not having to service these debts won't alone be enough to save Ukraine. But it is important in ensuring that, when they have reconquered their independence, Ukrainians won't be even more dependent on creditors or domestic oligarchs over whom they have no control.

David Broder: Some Western media talk about Ukrainians being "middle-class people just like us," sometimes counterposed to victims of war in other parts of the world. Can you give us a sense of what living standards were like for ordinary people even before last month?

Olexandr Kravchuk; What they say is not true. Ukraine was the northern part of the Global South and the poorest country in Europe, fighting for this place with Moldova.

On **[Infographic 1]** I provide some comparative data on our economic development.

Thus, in terms of national income per capita, Ukraine lags far behind the European Union, and even more so the United States. The latest data indicates the poverty of our people, with average wages below five hundred euros per month **[Infographic 2]**

After the beginning of the war in the East, the economic crisis of 2014, and the loss of markets, people's incomes have barely recovered in recent years. But even that level was still too low. The reasons for this were:

- Extracting wealth to offshore companies, often formed in the former Soviet industries following privatization.

- A focus on exports of raw materials (grain, metal, chemical industry).

- The wrong debt policy. Loans from the IMF were issued on terms which demanded that even the remnants of the welfare state be cut back. Payments simply to service the public debt have become one of the largest parts of the state's budget expenditure (amounting to 8.5 percent of the total in 2021).

- Lack of support for the Ukrainian high-tech products, in particular due to the unfair trade agreements with foreign partners (including the Association Agreement with the EU).

Olexandr Kravchuk is an economist and editor at *Commons: Journal for Social Criticism*, who has previously written about IMF conditions on loans to Ukraine. He died suddenly in July 2023.

The war that began in 2014 blocked the flow of investment, and only worsened the situation. Since then, we have also been restricted in terms of political participation. Socioeconomic protests were marginalized and were "out of place" during the war.

As a result, instead of fighting for a better future in Ukraine, Ukrainians went abroad en masse. Thus, according to the UN, in 2020 Ukraine ranked eighth in the world in terms of labor migration. Millions of Ukrainians have already left in recent years to eastern EU member states (e.g. Poland, Czech Republic). There, they replaced the labor force that left these countries looking for a better life in Germany, Great Britain, and other core countries. With this war, the EU is predicting as many as five

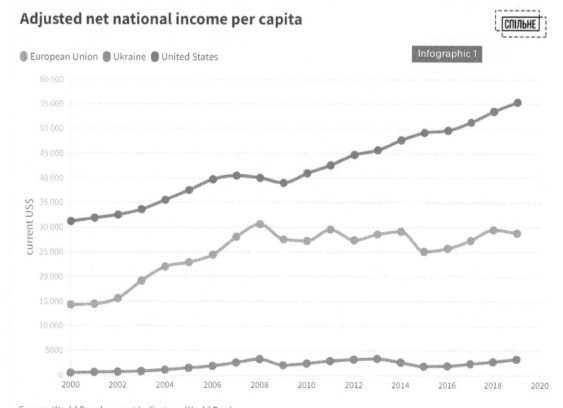

Adjusted net national income per capita

European Union Ukraine United States

Infographic 1

Source: World Development Indicators, World Bank

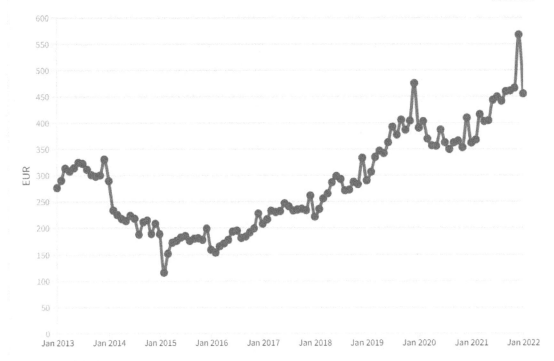

Source: State Statistics Service of Ukraine

million more people will arrive from Ukraine — a higher qualified labor force to integrate into European society.

DB: Over the last eight years, the IMF and World Bank did lend larger amounts to Ukraine. Were there "strings attached"? If Volodymyr Zelensky again seeks foreign loans, what resonance does the demand for debt relief have in Ukrainian society?

OK: The IMF and other financial institutions were drivers of so-called "market reforms" in Ukraine. We wrote about this in our project Alternative Mechanisms for the Socio-Economic Development of Ukraine. In 2015, I wrote an article for that pamphlet, regarding the origin of debt dependence and its negative impact on Ukraine. **[1]**

The last "victory" in this field was the changes in the energy market. In Ukraine, gas prices have increased ten times under IMF pressure since 2014. In November 2021, the Ukrainian government agreed with the IMF on the final deregulation and selling of gas produced in Ukraine, at high exchange prices. It could increase tariffs three or five times over during the war.

You may see a quick English translation of my latest infographic below **[Infographic 3]**:

We managed to promote the idea of revising debt policy in wider Ukrainian society. The proposal was picked up by different actors, including by nationalist forces. Nevertheless, the outside pressure was too strong, and Zelensky's new government was too weak to dare to break through it. After all, in this case it required a strong economic policy and the restoration of full-fledged sovereignty.

DB: In your petition you write that: "Chaotic borrowing and antisocial debt conditionality was a result of total oligarchisation: unwilling to fight the wealthy, the state rulers kept getting deeper in debt." Can you explain this — and does the high debt force the state to rely on oligarchic-private interests for infrastructure projects?

OK: This link between the weight of debt and reliance on private interests is rather indirect but still important. The argument that Ukraine has an excessive, bloated state has developed for a long time now. However, the share of national income that is distributed through taxation and budgeting in Ukraine is much less than in developed European countries.

Therefore, in conditions when most state-owned enterprises are privatized, Ukraine does not have the resources and capacities to develop infrastructure projects. Private capital in Ukraine focuses either on the commodity industries or the financial sector. This trend will be even more noticeable after the war, as private capital will be scared by instability in the region.

DB: *Many Western countries are already promising and delivering humanitarian aid to Ukraine. What is the specific importance of debt cancellation, firstly in fighting the war, and in allowing Ukrainians to shape their own future?*

OK: Sooner or later the war will end, and Ukraine will be left not only with bombed infrastructure but also with a large public debt.

The option of debt restructuring that took place last time is not suitable for the Ukrainian economy and is rather more attractive to creditors themselves. In 2015, some of the payments to commercial lenders were postponed for three years and 20 percent of the principal was written off. But what was the price for that? Ukraine was obliged to pay creditors 15 percent of its GDP increase over 3 percent, and 40 percent of each percent of its GDP increase over 4 percent. We could barely service our debt even before the war. The terms of the loan should be reviewed on a transparent basis.

DB: *What kind of mechanisms do you imagine would allow this demand to be fulfilled? What do you think of the precedent of West German debt cancellation in 1953?*

OK: I can't immediately suggest a debt review mechanism — in particular, because I am writing this under the sound of shelling.

But I am convinced that we can use, for example, the work of the Committee for the Abolition of Illegitimate Debt, as happened in Ecuador in 2008, when 70 percent of sovereign debt was declared illegal and the freed-up funds were used for economic development and welfare.

Today, it's difficult to think about what a peaceful life might be like for Ukraine. But we need to work on building an independent and socially just society. For this reason, the debt yoke should go in the dustbin of history — together with the army of Russian invaders.

Footnotes

[1] https://commons.com.ua/en/formuvannya-zalezhnosti/

10.03.2022
first published on *Jacobin*

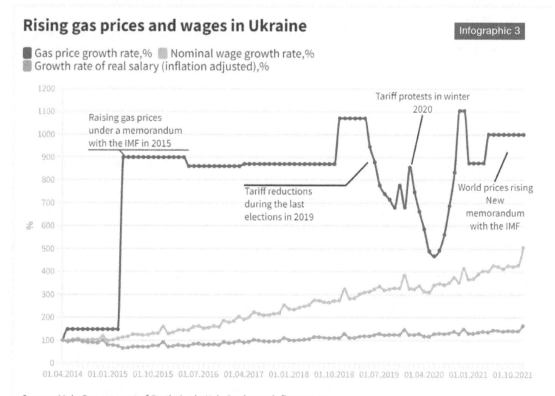

Rising gas prices and wages in Ukraine

Infographic 3

■ Gas price growth rate,% ■ Nominal wage growth rate,%
■ Growth rate of real salary (inflation adjusted),%

Raising gas prices under a memorandum with the IMF in 2015

Tariff protests in winter 2020

Tariff reductions during the last elections in 2019

World prices rising
New memorandum with the IMF

01.04.2014 01.01.2015 01.10.2015 01.07.2016 01.04.2017 01.01.2018 01.10.2018 01.07.2019 01.04.2020 01.01.2021 01.10.2021

Source: Main Department of Statistics in Kyiv Region, minfin.com.ua
On the example of wages and gas prices in the Kyiv region. (Kyivoblgaz Zbut LLC)

Ukrainian Economy and Society: Whither the (Postwar) Country?

Yuliya Yurchenko

Translated by **Yulia Kulish**

Intro: state of affairs, role of context

On February 24, 2022, when Russia yet again invaded Ukraine, the latter was already one of the poorest and most indebted countries in Europe, weathered by "transition to market" and associated "unintended consequences", numerous economic crises, and nearly 8 years of war with Russia and its proxies in Donbas and Crimea. Budgetary expenditure on arms, humanitarian needs, and medical needs (of the wounded) have grown exponentially. The scale of GDP contraction in April 2022 already was projected by the World Bank at 45%[1] while poverty rate projection for 2023 was at 58% year on year increase — and by now those actual figures will be higher despite recent optimistic figure updates. Money is needed to reconstruct Ukraine's homes and infrastructure; clean up, de-mine, and decontaminate cities and countryside. Ukraine is losing industrial and agricultural capacity, imports/exports are disrupted, and industries are leaking cadre due to displacement, refugee flows, impairments (physical and mental traumas), and death. Russian Federation will have to pay for the ruination; proposals and actions are being discussed yet the destiny of frozen assets, setting up repossessing/reparations mechanisms and more will not likely happen until Ukraine's victory. So, for now I want to focus on the losses Ukraine sustained to date set against the backdrop of constraints and opportunities set out in the post-war reconstruction plan presented in Lugano on 4-5 July 2022.

Social losses and economic de-development: war damage and (pre)war reforms

The full scale of losses will only be known upon full withdrawal of Russian troops from Ukraine's constitutional borders. The deep essence of concepts of "value" and "price" take on their most visceral forms when one stares in the face of a genocidal war carried out by a death cult regime. Ministry of Ecology and Natural Resources of Ukraine "estimated US$46 billion and still rising — includes direct war damage to air, forests, soil and water; remnants and pollution from the use of weapons and military equipment; and contamination from the shelling of thousands of facilities holding toxic and hazardous materials", The long term impact of losses to and of the ecosystems is impossible to quantify especially since Ukraine "contains habitats that are home to 35% of Europe's biodiversity, including 70,000 plant and animal species, many of them rare, relict, and endemic".

Ukraine needs external aid of roughly $4 billion per month to support the war effort and sustain essential public services while the need for budgetary support for 2023 is at $38 billion. The damage is so severe that even the usual advocates of market solutions to market and nonmarket problems e.g. Eichengreen and Rashkovan, call for grants and debt relief. By the end of 2022, the total amount of documented damage to Ukraine's infrastructure was estimated at $137.8 billion (at replacement cost). Since autumn 2022, all thermal and hydropower stations have been damaged, by February about a third of all power generation and distribution capacity is lost; "at least twice during these attacks, Ukrainian nuclear power plants lost connection to the grid, posing nuclear safety risks". Being a major global grain exporter,

Yuliya Yurchenko is a political economist, lecturer, Doctor of Philosophy (theory of international relations and political economy). Research interests: state-society-capital nexus and empire of capital, public services, commons, modes of governance.

the loss of 40% of production in 2022 is and will be felt in Ukraine and abroad, especially in low-income countries. Reduction in rural household food production of 25-38% (depending on proximity to frontlines) normally responsible for 25% of total country output is too felt in supply reduction and in price inflation[2]. In the early days of the invasion in 2022 "Russia must pay" project was launched to document war damages upon Ukrainian economy; the results and analysis are published on damaged.in.ua website and are updated regularly[3].

Ukraine in and postwar rebuilding tasks sit against the challenges of financial, demographic, and institutional capacity being uncertain. Further complications arise when we assess the "externalities" of the war alongside the "unintended consequences" of the market reform Ukraine went through since 1991 (corruption and oligarchs as part and parcel but not the only ill of it), is implementing now and plans more of after the war (see Lugano plan and labour reform below). In the process of "transition to market" since 1991 Ukraine has suffered large scale de-development i.e., its foundational economy, its public services and infrastructure have deteriorated and suffered from systemic and chronic underfunding. This resulted, among other, into socialisation and individualisation of costs of meeting the needs previously catered by those state funded services and/or those services altogether lacking or being of reduced supply with notable regional variegation. Discursive normalisation

Table 1. Total damages, monetary terms (Dec '22-Jan '23 at replacement cost), $bn

Housing stock	54	Culture, sport, tourism	2.2
Infrastructure	35.6	Healthcare	1.7
Assets of enterprises	13	Administrative building	0.8
Education	8.6	Electronic communications	0.6
Energy (open source data calculation, to be corrected in future)	6.8	Social sphere	0.2
Agriculture and land resources	6.6	Financial sphere	0.1
Transport	2.9	Demining	
Trade	2.4	Ecology (emissions damage, not direct to any assets)	14
Utilities	2.3		
TOTAL:			137.8

Source: KSE (2023)

of those changes and responsibilisation of the populace for this combination of state and market failures became an additional ideological stumbling bloc in the way of increasingly agitated civil society's efforts to address the symptomatic results of those failures e.g. demands for full private healthcare provision instead of fully deployed and state funded system. While these problems often get blamed on mismanagement, corruption and embezzlement, they have more to do with a combination of the "costs" of the EU rapprochement reform, budgetary constraints, IMF Structural Adjustment Loans conditionality, and similar limitations on fiscal policy choices that straightjacket even the most well-meaning state administrators as is evidenced by similar experiences of numerous other countries.

It is hard to be precise about the social losses and damages too, not unlike economic albeit for different reasons yet it is the individual struggles that are most revealing of the gaps in state and market provision like, tell us where the rebuilding effort will be most needed. The compound and complex effects of the 9 year-long war especially for IDPs and refugees reveal pre-existing capitalist and patriarchal reproductive inequalities which have been exacerbated by displacement with variegated effects and severity. Access to adequate resources (inc. cash) and (child)care, suitable & stable housing are acute issues for IDPs (and also those who stayed at home). Real estate and particularly rental markets are poorly regulated, rental prices in cities considered relatively safe have magnified overnight while availability is low. This leads to three forms of displacement: "displacement caused by the dangers of war, displacement caused by destruction of homes, and displacement caused by the rent market itself". A comprehensive state funded housing programme is needed which may be tricky if the role and function of the state in the Recovery Plan is not reimagined. Most Ukrainians can't afford inflated mortgage and rental market properties, nor to upgrade the old Soviet stock that was depleted by 3 decades of poor municipal investment and recently the wars.

Schools and kindergartens being bombed, education and care for children provision are extremely challenging which is made worse by pre-existing problems in those sectors — from chronic underfunding and understaffing to low wages of the employees and parents struggling financially, especially in single parent (mainly mother) households.

The situation with employment and income amidst displacement, shelling, and inflation is too highly challenging. Accurate data is lacking but what is clear is that things are getting worse. Djankov, S. and O. Blinov (17 Nov 2022) use wage payments data from one of Ukraine's largest commercial banks to get a picture:

"Since the start of the war, nominal wages have managed modest growth, amounting to 3% by end-October. However, wages dropped 11% in real terms over the January to October period and their decline has accelerated to 18% in the past month". Moreover, "13% of hired em-

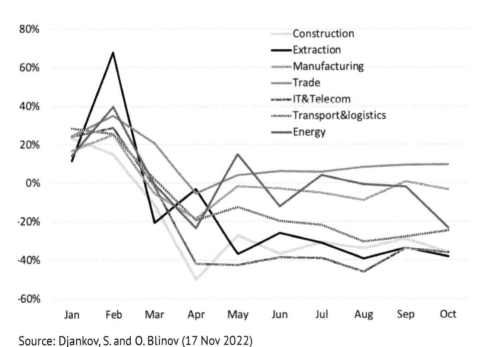

Figure 1: Productive economy average nominal wage, year-on-year change in 2022

Source: Djankov, S. and O. Blinov (17 Nov 2022)

ployees have lost their job since the start of the war and there is evidence of increasing job losses."

This is amidst YOY inflation in 2022 alone going to 26.6% from 10% end of 2021; in pre-pandemic 2019 it was 4%. To top it all, instead of protecting the rights of people in wartime, antilabour laws in mid-2022 stripped some 70% of workers of labour code protection. According to labour lawyer and the leader of the Sotsialnyi Rukh organisation Vitaliy Dudin, the changes "affect workplaces with hundreds of workers, including public sector jobs at risk of austerity policies, such as hospitals, railway depots, post offices and infrastructure maintenance".

Jobs are being lost, savings are depleted, credit cards maxed out; many struggle to service their debts, and even more will struggle having access to credit finance now and in the future, due to access criteria/costs and availability alike. This, never minds the unfairness of household debt accumulation, is why this debt must be written off as part of the (post)war recovery approach — an economy cannot run on a mix of good will of increasingly poorer friends/relatives and sporadic local and foreign donations to food, meds, and clothes collections. A set of comprehensive policies must be developed, a complete overhaul of the problems that existed before the 2014 and 2022 invasions which exacerbated those problems but did not create them.

Debt politics amidst socio-economic upheaval and erosion of sovereignty

Chaotic borrowing and debt explosion in Ukraine over the years was partly a result of oligarchic state capture and kleptocracy. IFI loans were issued under conditions of social spending cuts, economising on vital needs. The country's debt demand context was characterised by the loss of a real economic base at a rate disproportionate to the growth required to maintain the health of the economy or honour debts, state or private. Debt increased up to 5 times denominated in UAH mostly due to dollarisation, Euroization, and high value-added goods import dependency. Until the summer 2022 Ukraine adhered to its debt obligations. Between February 24 to October 2, 2022, "the amount of funds paid by the government for the repayment of domestic debt instruments by UAH 54,093.9 million exceeds the amount of funds raised in the state budget at auctions for the sale of government domestic loan bonds". Clearly an alternative form of financing is needed — more grants, not more loans concealed as aid.

A temporary suspension of debt servicing has been agreed between Ukraine, The Paris Club and G7 on July 20, 2022, and signed on Sept 14, 2022, for 1 year as of Aug 1, 2022, with a possible extension for one more year (decision affecting about 75% of all foreign debt) — not least due to multipartite international civil society campaigning. Yet this is insufficient; not least since IMF debt conditionality is firmly in place and debt surcharges are still to be paid.

In Ukraine's case, historically conditioned relationship with EU/western partners and Russia (mainly), economic and geopolitical, add extra dimensions of simultaneous complexity and fragility, via debt, trade arrears, and import/export dependencies. Debt as an instrument of external control and expropriation of national wealth, combined with the modern system of taxation and trade regimes is a powerful diluter of the decision-making autonomy fundamental for any meaningful exercise of political sovereignty. Debt leads to "alienation of the state," that is, the national state ceases to be an autonomous agent of authority and representation of its people's will. Ukraine had to engage in war bonds sale and utilise numerous rapid financing mechanisms available internationally to fund the war effort where aid was insufficient, each coming with its conditions and more constraints.

Reconstruction plan and EU prospects — what can make it a success?

In Lugano, Switzerland on July 4-5, 2022, the Ukraine Recovery Conference URC2022 outlined dimensions for Ukraine's revival which sounds promising yet the means don't match the aims i.e. the state will struggle to finance or attract enough private investment/direct it where it is most needed — the whole of $750 billion of it so far. Discussions revolve around it being modelled on the Marshall Plan which was a success due to cash grants and loans and recipient discretion in spending. The European countries often used this money to buy essential goods like wheat and oil and to reconstruct factories and housing. A like plan for Ukraine would need to be (re) designed and executed in alignment with the best practice and standards of EU labour right, public services and environmental protection; for that to happen a number of changes I outline below need to occur.

Ukraine's extraordinary situation presents a case for large-scale multi-faceted international assistance, state and household debt cancellation, and conditionality of new loans rewriting to facilitate "fiscal activism" i.e., measures aimed at stabilising business cycles via discretionary use of fiscal policy. Austerity is uneconomical and unecological even at peacetime, let alone at war. What is needed is full state-funded (re)development of public services and care economy — with a radical internalisation of positive externalities into assessment of state investment returns — which must become mainstream political discourse in Ukraine and among its international partners. The state in Ukraine is not bloated, unlike its stereotypical perception, but on the contrary — "the share of national income distributed through taxation and budgetary allocation in Ukraine is much smaller than in advanced economies of the EU". State was the key agent in rebuilding much of Europe, Japan and South Korea after World War II - the "developmental state" was elaborated as a concept, and now is the time to return to it as "free" markets fail especially at wartime. Principles of the European Green Deal and beyond with the state at the centre of recovery is what is needed.

IMF and other creditors are needed as sources of financing. But it is state institutions that carry out the recovery and should have "the ownership of the reconstruction process". Moreover, the key role of civil society (NGOs and trade unions, the latter being often left out) delivering where state and markets alike failed since 2014 must be acknowledged, scaffolded, and financed by the state instead of international crowd-funders — such polycentric form of the governance (Ostrom) and the state as institutional network can deliver the rebuilding Ukrainians envisage; it can also allow the principles of deep sustainability reflected in the Lugano Recovery Plan become a reality by treating economy as a socio-ecological system rather than a sum of economic fragments. Local enterprises should have priority over the foreign. The economic policy consensus has shifted globally to favour (post)Keynesian vision of state-led investment in own economies to boost confidence and kick-start the multiplier effect, while SAPs have been criticised by IMF own research as limiting on macroeconomic growth, the de facto relationships with the Fund's borrowers have not changed, they since were renamed "conditionality" but in essence have not become less rigid, increased in fact; those debts and their conditionalities must be cancelled.

Ukraine will need green/low carbon job creation (e.g., care economy, arts, education, environmental preservation & sustainable R&D, etc.), just transition, and energy democracy which will maximise possibilities for its economic self-sufficiency and reduce import dependency of key industries. Job creation is key as millions of Ukrainians work abroad seasonally, more now have left the country etc — by 2017 7-9 million left the country to work abroad, 3.3 million between 2011-21 alone, "while their families remained in Ukraine. The inflow of remittances to Ukraine in 2020 reached $12.1 billion". While those transactions support Ukraine's economy, they are hardly an indicator of good quality of life for average citizens whose lives are destabilised. In 2021 alone 660,302 persons left the country amidst challenges exacerbated by the COVID-19 pandemic. Vast numbers fled the country since the invasion of Feb 24, 2022. Conditions must be created for people to be able to come back and will need to range from infrastructure and (social) housing (re)building (including whole towns in some cases) and sustainable job creation across Ukraine. Surveys, multiple journalistic articles and reports, and anecdotal evidence all point out to Ukrainians' will to return to Ukraine once (1) it is safe and (2) once they have somewhere to go back to, many return even without certain jobs nor survival guarantees.

EU integration can become a saving grace for Ukraine's economy or it can become a force for further de-development and peripherilisation. Lessons from experiences of other economically weaker and newer member states here is key and it has been observed that integration processes are a game rigged against EU periphery countries. Ukraine's situation is extraordinary not least due to its membership path laid through the debris of a genocidal war for which rapprochement with the EU and NATO were used as a pretext. Moreover, from the outset the demographic, economic, institutional, and ecological tasks at hand are stupendous even judged by standards of an advanced peacetime economy. This sets context for equally extraordinary arrangement of the rules of engagement of which many are already underway; yet many are bigger in aims than in means proposed. For recovery to become what was outlined in Lugano, a fundamental rewriting of the global debt and policy conditionality regime, the "black holes" of offshore, tax avoidance and evasion including transfer pricing must disappear. Further, a proposal can be made of a potential plan-case to follow for construction for similar economies globally. We need to think beyond Ukraine, we need to think Ukraine as part of the global economy, and we need to be thinking alternative economic systems altogether built by and for noospheric societies — societies of the era of reason where wars, poverty, and ecocide are made impossible by design.

Footnotes

[1] This has been updated for a better projection since yet there are few reasons for optimism.

[2] This includes "approximately 85 percent of fruit and vegetable production, 81 percent of milk and around half of livestock production" (FAO 2023: 1).

[3] The data is collected to be used (1) "to document war crimes and human rights violations; (2) for the formation of claims against the Russian Federation in international courts for compensation for damage caused: lawsuits for international courts require aggregate evidence and a register of damaged objects in accordance of the methodology of estimating; (3) for individual compensation; (3) to receive war reparations and compensa-

tions for damage from the aggressor for the reconstruction of Ukraine".

The article is based on a chapter from the book "Europe and the War in Ukraine: From Russian Aggression to a New Eastern Policy".

08.06.2023

Principles for Ukraine's Post-war Reconstruction in the Energy System. Workers and Social Movements Approach

Simon Pirani

It is difficult for all of us to talk about post-war reconstruction when the war is raging. Every day this means not only deaths and injuries, but also the destruction of civilian infrastructure, including power stations and boiler houses.

This winter, Ukrainians will be trying to protect themselves from bombs and bullets, but also trying to stay warm and healthy in the face of disruptions to gas, heat and electricity supplies. But even under these circumstances, discussion has begun about post-war reconstruction, in the first place between the Ukrainian government and European governments at the Lugano conference. They are making plans for the long term.

The labour movement, and social movements, need an approach to these issues that takes the side of working people and of society, as opposed to economic or political elites. I will suggest some principles on which the labour movement and social movements in Ukraine could base their approach to the energy system.

1. Energy should be supplied mainly from renewable sources.

Society internationally needs an energy transition – that is, a transition to a system without fossil fuels, centred on electricity networks, with the electricity generated from renewable sources such as solar, wind and wave power. In Ukraine, there is also some potential for biofuels made from agricultural waste.

I am sure everyone present knows why this is: because global heating could seriously damage human society, and the chief cause of global heating is the burning of fossil fuels. For the last 30 years, the world's most powerful governments have gone to great lengths to delay the energy transition while simultaneously pretending to deal with the problem. The labour movement and social movements need to advocate a transition that serves the interests of society, not capital.

Two points to make about Ukraine specifically.

- Coal has historically been central, in the Donbas in particular. Coal use has been falling since 2016, mainly due to Russian military aggression. Now, political forces in the Donbas are discussing a future without coal. For example in the recent open letter by the Mayors of Myrnohrad, Chervonohrad and other towns. I hope that the labour movement and social movements will engage in this discussion.

- Gas has also played a key role. The government has sought to reduce dependence on Russian gas, and there have been no direct imports since 2015. However, in Ukraine, as elsewhere, gas companies make the false argument that gas is part of the solution to the problem of greenhouse gas emissions, because it produces energy with fewer emissions than coal. Actually, it's part of the problem. The energy transition means moving away from gas.

2. It is in society's interests to cut the flow of energy through technological systems.

To understand this, we should, first, forget the idea of "energy demand". People do not want "energy". They want the things that it provides — heat, light, electricity to run computers, the ability to travel from place to place, and so on. These things can be provided, using far less energy than is used now, by making better use of technologies that have existed for decades.

Simon Pirani is a socialist writer and historian. His books include *Burning Up: a global history of fossil fuel consumption* (2018) and *Change in Putin's Russia: power, money and people* (2010). He has written widely on energy issues in Ukraine, especially about the gas industry. He is a lifelong activist in the labour movement and former editor of the British mineworkers' union journal.

An obvious example is heat for people's homes. In Ukraine, this comes mainly from gas boilers, or by district heating systems based on combined heat and power plants.

Governments, not only in Ukraine but across Europe, can start tackling this problem now. First, we need insulation, to reduce the amount of heat needed. Second, we need electric heat pumps that are four or five times more efficient than gas boilers. This would keep people warm, reduce the amount of gas needed and cut greenhouse gas emissions. These technologies are very simple, although retrofitting them to old buildings can be tricky.

These are short-term measures. In the long term, engineers see the creation of integrated urban energy systems as the priority. In such systems, there would be multiple inputs of renewably-produced electricity. These would be integrated with a range of electricity storage facilities, from hydro storage to electric vehicles. These systems can be integrated, but also decentralised. This makes them more compatible with collective, non-state forms of social organisation that socialists favour.

Non-governmental organisations in Ukraine who favour such systems have advanced the idea of "energy freedom", that is, "the greatest possible freedom for citizens, organisations and communities to produce energy and manage it in their own economies". In my view, socialists should take part in the discussion about what this means in practice.

3. We should demand that fuels and electricity are treated as services, as rights for all, not as commodities.

Now, after decades of neoliberalism, oil, gas and electricity are treated as commodities not only for international trade but, in many countries, in retail markets.

In Ukraine there is a public service obligation on companies to supply electricity and gas to households at fixed prices. There are discussions at government level about how to change this system, in the name of reducing inefficiencies.

It's a basic principle for the labour movement that these changes should not be made at the expense of households. However, we should also go further, and challenge the notion that fuels, or electricity, are commodities to be bought and sold.

4. We should favour technologies that are compatible with our aims of social justice, and resist the imposition of technologies that serve the state and capital.

This is relevant to post-war reconstruction.

The EU has its "green new deal", that involves a limited shift to renewable energy supply technologies, but that protects powerful energy corporations and liberalised markets. Many Ukrainian politicians are happy with this political framework and some of the technological choices it implies. This takes them along paths that I believe the labour movement and civil society should oppose.

For example, the EU is discussing plans to produce electricity from big wind and solar farms in Ukraine, and use it to produce hydrogen for export. The hydrogen would be produced by electrolysis of water, a very energy-intensive process.

This is greenwash at its worst. Clearly, Ukraine needs electricity from wind and solar to end its reliance on coal and gas. To use it, instead, to produce hydrogen for export would be a form of neo-colonialism. I hope the labour movement and civil society, in Europe and Ukraine, will block this plan.

Another live political issue is whether new nuclear plants, specifically Khmelnitsky-3 and Khmelnitsky-4, should be built. This is in the interests of some Ukrainian politicians and business elites, but not in society's interests. It is feasible to aim for a system that provides the electricity that Ukraine needs from renewable sources, without new nuclear. So investment in it will obstruct this aim.

Of course behind this there are broader arguments about whether and how nuclear power should be part of post-fossil-fuel energy systems at all. I am not enthusiastic about nuclear power, because it is by its nature closely bound up with powerful state and military structures. By contrast, decentralised renewable technologies are by their nature compatible with collective, egalitarian ways of organising society.

15.12.2022

Together in Trouble: Social Policy for a Just Reconstruction in Ukraine

Natalia Lomonosova

The war bitterly hit the whole population of Ukraine. Many people lost their jobs and left their homes. According to the September survey of the sociological group Rating, only 61% of Ukrainians remained at their job positions, 36% of whom worked full-time[1]. According to World Bank estimates, as of August 2022, about 817,000 residential buildings were damaged, 38% of which — were beyond repair. In other words, millions of Ukrainians ended up vulnerable.

The war put on verge of survival a significant part of people who belonged to the vulnerable, poorly protected categories of the population. In addition, some social infrastructure is damaged or destroyed[2], and the workload of institutions providing social services has increased tremendously due to the flow of displaced persons. The social protection system is also overloaded, especially against the background of the shortages in budget revenues. Therefore, systemic social support is not only a priority issue but is also, so to speak, under question.

In this article, I will define the trends observed in Ukrainian social policy in the pre-war years since they demonstrate the government's vision of social support policy. Next, I will consider the existing state's proposals in the field of social policy and analyze the politics behind such a vision. Finally, I will sketch the alternative approaches to post-war social policy and the reasons for the social policy being essential to the reconstruction.

Social protection during the war

The system of Ukrainian social protection was not ready for such a challenge as a full-scale invasion. In July, the recovery plan for the Ukrainian social protection sphere was presented in Lugano. Its authors attribute this situation to the obsolescence and "sovietness" of the Ukrainian social protection system: it is excessive and promises citizens benefits that the state cannot guarantee in practice.

Undoubtedly, every government puts the burden of the problems on its predecessor. However, why turn to such a distant past as the Soviet Union, having a thirty-year story of reductions in spending on the social sphere, privatization, and the decline of public social infrastructure? At the same time, it is obvious the authorities have no intention of departing from this course.

Since the beginning of the full-scale war, the government has announced and implemented several measures to stabilize the well-being of people. But many led to a reduction in labor rights and the rights of trade unions, limiting the possibility of receiving unemployment benefits. For example, the registered unemployed will be engaged in community service[3] with payment not lower than the minimum wage if they don't get a job during 30 days. However, those who refuse to serve the community will lose the status of unemployed and benefit payments.

Moreover, the government announced the development of the Social Code aimed at "inventorizing information on the existing obligations for social payments of the state" and bringing them in line with the state's financial capabilities. In addition, Law 2620 has liquidated the Social Insurance Fund. Pension Fund received its budget and part of the functions while its expenses and employees were significantly reduced. Therefore, the functioning of the social insurance system is a big issue.

A significant part of the measures taken by the government during the war and proposed in the draft recovery plan is not only and not so much justified by the chal-

Natalia Lomonosova is a sociologist who researches and analyzes social protection and labor policies and an analyst of the *Cedos* think tank, where she is involved in research in the fields of social policy.

lenges that the war itself brings. They are a continuation of the political course that has been here for a long time in the field of social policy (as well as in related areas, for instance, in health care). Such a political course has been called neoliberalism for several decades. However, let us not talk of the very ideology of neoliberalism. Instead, I suggest outlining the neoliberal traces in particular political programs.

An old enemy of neoliberalism

What is commonly known as the welfare state is an old enemy and target of neoliberalism. European social policies arose and thrived precisely in the post-war period. Although, in the 1970s, the oil crisis and economic recession made representatives of the neoliberal wing complain about "high" spending on social programs and support of the population slowing down the pace of economic growth.

The history of social policy in Ukraine has different origins than in the West. However, in the 1990s, we got on the train to a market economy. The economic recession of the first decade and full-scale privatization immediately led to reducing spending on the social sphere and the deterioration of social infrastructure, especially in rural areas. For example, the first two decades of independence brought a decrease in the number of kindergartens by almost two-thirds. At the same time, international donors and creditors encouraged the reduction of budget expenditures in the social sphere (or, as it was often formulated, "effective use of resources"). Globalization and the pursuit of investors also become a separate incentive for systematic attempts to limit labor rights

and social guarantees, as well as to create more attractive tax conditions for businesses to retain capital.

From universalism to supporting the poorest

What does the neoliberal course look like in the Ukrainian social sphere? On the one hand, it is based on intentions *to reduce the spending on social protection*; on the other hand, *to change the very nature of the social policy*.

How does the reduction of spending work? To obtain a benefit, you must demonstrate that you need assistance, that is, verify your income. However, the income threshold is very low.

For instance, let us consider the conditions for identifying a family as low-income so that it can receive assistance. As of November 2022, to get financial aid, a family of two adults and one child under the age of 6 must declare that their average monthly total income for the last 6 months is less than UAH 29,474 (about UAH 4,912 per month)[4]. Moreover, not only does income affect the decision to aid, but also other factors. For example, the reply may be negative if one or both adults have not worked, studied full-time, or been employed for the past three months. In addition, control measures are very strict so that those who are not entitled to assistance do not receive it.

Also, *reductions in existing social programs take place*. As I already mentioned, the government intends to modify the existing social obligations of the state to reduce everything that allegedly "does not correspond to financial possibilities." In addition, they announced the "transformation of the extensive system of social payments into universal social assistance," which will be targeted at the poorest. Such a social protection course no longer provides, for example, financial aid to all single mothers. Instead, only those passing an income test — the poorest — will get this aid. Therefore, in fact, *citizens are gradually deprived of any universal rights to support.*

In terms of *changes in the very nature of the social policy,* we can see *attempts to replace the entities that provide social services and their financing scheme.* Thus, the 2019 reform aims to create a market of social services, with private service-providing institutions contesting state and communal ones. However, the state must finance the services provided at the expense of the state, not the institution. Therefore, it follows the logic of medical reform, where the money comes with a patient, and hospitals transform into enterprises earning money to exist.

The same proposals we may find in the field of pension provision. Draft reconstruction plan and the specialized committee of the Verkhovna Rada called pension reform an "objective necessity," not hurrying to implement it before the war. It is about abandoning the solidarity pension system in favor of a mixed one by introducing individual pension plans and partially privatizing the pension provision.

To sum up, apart from the reduction of funding, everything turns into a source of profit.

In addition, while there are supposedly no financial sources to support the social security system, nobody mentions increasing the taxation of business profits, large corporations, and enterprises, introducing a more progressive tax rate. On the contrary, in times of war, the state makes concessions to businesses, in particular in the field of taxes. At the same time, the tax burden on employees does not change. *That is, the social reproduction of the labor force that businesses use increasingly relies on the labor force itself.*

Solidarity or atomization?

Why is such a course dangerous? In most states with a developed social policy, part of the support programs varies depending on the recipient's income level. However, the question is what amount of public goods (or, as we say — services) is available to all citizens as a *universal right,* regardless of their income. For example, in terms of ensuring guaranteed free access to kindergartens, schooling and health services, child benefit payments, etc.

The less universal the various government assistance programs are, the closer they are to supporting only the poorest and the less support they usually have among the taxpayers. For example, if only the poorest are entitled to assistance, the average person may feel hopeless in receiving aid, even though their situation may

be difficult. So, why pay social security contributions for something you can't count on? *People are less willing to invest in something they most likely will not get any benefit from. Thus, in the future, social protection expenditures will naturally decline even more.* It means that the number of active support programs will also decrease.

In addition, such an approach *stigmatizes the recipients,* as they seem to disconnect from the rest of society. Being under maximum pressure to enter the labor market as soon as possible also may encourage the recipients to agree on any job under any conditions. It further deepens their insecurity — this time, in the workplace. People who cannot enter the labor market for various reasons are considered pests and dependents since the rest of the taxpayers do not receive anything from the state but anyway have to support them.

Due to the gradual reduction of state funding, *the quality of the public goods provided by communal and state facilities may decline.* Therefore, wealthier people are less inclined to use their services, preferring the private ones: schools, medical facilities, care facilities, etc. Public service providers and their clients are even more stigmatized. Finally, support for spending on the welfare state is decreasing: after all, why finance something that "we" do not use and that is of lower quality?

From a political perspective, the structural, *tectonic changes in political consciousness* are dangerous. I mean *the individualization of social risks* due to the limitation of the range of recipients. Individual pension plans, where a person's well-being essentially depends on the success of their investments in the stock market, are an illustrative model of this trend. As a result, a person associates themselves with business, an investor, rather than with fellow citizens. It undermines the feeling of intergenerational support and *leads to the individualization of social consciousness when everyone is on their own, and the state will help only in the worst case.*

Is this the kind of society we aspire to, especially after the war? Why should we move toward greater individualization and atomization while experiencing unprecedented unity?

Social policy of a solidarity society

The war influenced everyone, but some suffered disproportionately greater losses, for instance, people who were already in a tough situation. For them, problems have only intensified and overlapped. So how to overcome this situation and develop united and solidarity society?

It would be fair to demand higher income taxation and redistribution of income to implement generous social policies and universal social protection programs. There is no other effective way of supporting those who have lost their homes and jobs. We must not only stand in solidarity in the face of the enemy's army, but also internally, among ourselves. Otherwise, our collective strength will be exhausted, as everyone will focus on their own survival.

It is not only about political visions of what our society can be. There are also *pragmatic considerations* behind this. Equal societies with generous social policies, where everyone agrees to contribute to the common good and gets benefits afterward, are happier, healthier, and *more stable.* After the war, we must not allow internal political instability, as economic, survival, and dignified life issues can deepen social divisions. It also applies to the reintegration of the currently occupied territories and, above all, to the territories occupied since 2014. A generous and universal social policy can become one of the instruments for the social consolidation and reintegration of those living in uncontrolled areas for years.

Social policy as a system of support for the poorest cannot face the challenges of war and post-war reconstruction without leading to increased inequality and atomization of society. We need a universal and solidarity social policy covering every group and providing minimum decent living standards for everyone. Such a system can help people feel included in a network of social solidarity they can count on.

Footnotes

[1] According to the survey, the IPDs, the women residing in Eastern regions, and the poorest of the East are most exposed to job loss. The survey is representative of the adult population of Ukraine. It does not include residents of temporarily occupied territories and residents of areas with no Ukrainian mobile communication at the time of the survey. Therefore, we can assume that the overall situation is even worse.

[2] World Bank analysts estimated the damage caused to the infrastructure of Ukrainian social protection (boarding facilities, institutions providing social services to the population, etc.) at 164.4 million dollars. As of August, 56 such buildings were damaged or destroyed. In addition, 64 of more than 470 service centers of the Pension Fund suffered significant damage, as well as 19 of the 158 offices of the Social Insurance Fund.

[3] Community service is defensive or serves to eliminate emergencies.

[4] It is the right of the families whose average monthly total income over the last 6 months is lower than the subsistence minimum. In 2022, this minimum accounts for 45% of the subsistence minimum established for this category; for persons who have lost working capacity and persons with disabilities –100%; for children — up to 130%. For example, as of July, for an able-bodied person, the subsistence minimum level is UAH 1,170 per month or EUR 29 (45% of UAH 2,481); for children under the age of 6 — UAH 2,861 or EUR 71.

28.11.2022

Milton Keynes UK
Ingram Content Group UK Ltd.
UKHW051819031123
431812UK00006B/270